Accounting Work Skills

Workbook

AAT Diploma Pathway Unit 31

Michael Fardon

Roger Petheram

osborne
BOOKS

Published by Osborne Books Limited
Unit 1B Everoak Estate
Bromyard Road
Worcester WR2 5HP
Tel 01905 748071
Email books@osbornebooks.co.uk
Website www.osbornebooks.co.uk

Design by Richard Holt
Cover image from Getty Images

Printed by CPI Antony Rowe Limited, Chippenham

British Library Cataloguing in Publication Data
A catalogue record for this book is available from the British Library

ISBN 978 1905777 037

Contents

Acknowledgements

The authors wish to thank the following for their help with the editing and production of this book: Sarah Fardon, Mike Gilbert, Rosemarie Griffiths and Jon Moore. The publisher would also like to thank Debbie Board for helping to produce the computer accounting activities.

The publisher is indebted to the Association of Accounting Technicians for its generous help and advice to our authors and editors during the preparation of this text, and for permission to reproduce extracts from the Specifications for the Diploma Pathway and the sample Unit 31 Simulation.

Authors

Michael Fardon has extensive teaching experience of a wide range of banking, business and accountancy courses at Worcester College of Technology. He now specialises in writing business and financial texts and is General Editor at Osborne Books. He is also an educational consultant and has worked extensively in the areas of vocational business curriculum development.

Roger Petheram has lectured at Worcester College of Technology on a wide range of accounting, business and management courses for a number of years. He previously worked as a senior accountant for the Health Service. He is currently senior editor for accounting texts at Osborne Books, with particular responsibility for the AAT Series.

Introduction

Accounting Work Skills Workbook is designed to be used alongside Osborne Books' *Accounting Work Skills Tutorial* and is ideal for student use in the classroom, at home and on distance learning courses. Both the *Tutorial* and the *Workbook* are designed for students preparing for assessment for the AAT Diploma Pathway Unit 31 'Accounting Work Skills', either at Certificate or Advanced Certificate level.

Accounting Work Skills Workbook is divided into two sections: Workbook Activities and Practice Simulations.

Workbook Activities

Workbook activities are self-contained exercises which are designed to be used to supplement the activities in the tutorial text. The computerised accounting exercises for Chapters 12 to 15 have been specifically written in the style of the second part of the AAT Simulation. Osborne Books is grateful to the AAT who provided very useful advice in the compilation of these exercises.

Practice Simulations

The AAT Unit 31 Simulation, at the time of writing, is in three parts. Parts 1 and 2 are time constrained, whereas Part 3 (which includes areas such as Health & Safety and Working with Others) is a 'take-away' project which has to be completed within the space of one month. The first practice Simulation is adapted from the AAT sample simulation and the second Simulation follows the same model. The more that students are able to practise simulation tasks, the more competent and confident they will become.

downloadable spreadsheets

Unit 31 requires competence in the use of computer spreadsheets. These are used widely in this text. Suitable files can be downloaded from the Resources Section of www.osbornebooks.co.uk These files will help students tackling the following activities and Practice Simulations:

- Activities 6.5, 6.7 and 6.8 – Enigma Electronics Limited
- Practice Simulation 1, Tasks 1, 3 and 4 – Ripley Manufacturing Limited
- Practice Simulation 2, Tasks 1.1, 1.3 and 1.4 – Iosis Electronics Limited

answers

The answers to the tasks and practice simulations in the *Workbook* are available in a separate *Tutor Pack*. Contact the Osborne Books Sales Office on 01905 748071 for details or obtain an order form from www.osbornebooks.co.uk

www.osbornebooks.co.uk

Visit the Osborne Books website, which contains Resources sections for tutors and students. These sections provide a wealth of free material, including downloadable documents and layouts and assistance with other areas of study. See the section on downloadable spreadsheets on the previous page.

Workbook activities

Element 31.1: Present financial data for internal and external use

This section contains activities which are suitable for use with Chapters 1 to 9 of *Accounting Work Skills Tutorial* from Osborne Books.

Element 31.1 is very much the 'number crunching' area of the Unit, and it is essential that students obtain plenty of practice in the type of tasks they may encounter in Part 1 of the Simulation. Chapter 6 offers particular challenges in this area, and students must ensure that they know how to consolidate financial information and present the results. The spreadsheets used in some of the activities for this Chapter are available for download free of charge from the Resources Section of www.osbornebooks.co.uk

As noted in *Accounting Work Skills Tutorial,* Chapter 2, which deals with financial statements, is optional, and will not be assessed in the Simulation. The subject area, however, is important to Unit 31, and if in doubt, students should consult with their tutor about tackling the questions on pages 14 and 15 of this workbook.

8

1 MANAGEMENT ACCOUNTING – COSTS AND CODING

1.1 In the first list below, five items of information are shown, labelled A to E. These are examples of the kind of information which managers of a business might find useful. In the second list below, six possible management tasks are shown, labelled (i) to (vi).

For each of the six management tasks, list the items of information from the first list, A to E, which managers may find useful for that task. There may be more than one item for each task and the items may be used more than once.

A   Rates of pay for different grades of labour

B   Sales forecasts for a product for the next year at different selling prices

C   The total cost of repairs to machinery in the last year

D   Estimated prices of raw materials for the next year

E   The amount of time lost during the last year due to machine breakdowns

(i)   Deciding on selling prices for products in the future

(ii)   Budgeting for the cost of production for the next year

(iii)   Checking monthly totals of wages

(iv)   Deciding whether to scrap old machines and buy new ones

(v)   Preparing a budget for the next quarter, to make sure sufficient cash is available when needed

(vi)   Finding ways to reduce costs within the business.

1.2 For each of the management tasks (i) to (vi) in Activity 1.1 (above), state which of the following functions of management would best describe that task:

Decision-making

Planning

Control

1.3 Which of the phrases below describe features of financial accounting and which describe features of management accounting?

(a)   reports relating to what has happened in the past

(b)   may be required by law

(c)   gives estimates of costs and income for the future

(d)   may be made public

(e)   gives up-to-date reports which can be used for controlling the business

(f)   is used by people outside the business

(g)   is designed to meet requirements of people inside the business

(h)   shows details of the costs of materials, labour and expenses

(i)   records accurate amounts, not estimates

1.4   A friend of yours, Rob Willis, started his own business several years ago, making small toys from moulded plastics. The business has expanded rapidly and now employs 8 production workers, 4 people in selling and distribution and 3 office workers. A book-keeper records all the business transactions and, at the end of the financial year, the financial accounts are prepared by an accountant. Up to now, Rob Willis has managed the business fairly successfully, making decisions on a day-to-day basis. So that he can improve his management skills he asks your advice about making use of management accounting information.

Write a note to Rob Willis explaining how management accounting differs from financial accounting, and suggesting ways in which management accounting information might help him in managing his business.

1.5   The following are items of expenditure incurred in a company which manufactures clothing. Write them in three columns, headed 'Materials costs', 'Labour costs' and 'Expenses'.

(a)   Premium for the insurance of buildings

(b)   Salaries of the office staff

(c)   The cost of zip fasteners

(d)   The cost of electricity

(e)   Wages of storekeepers

(f)   Overtime payments for machinists

(g)   The cost of a consignment of blue denim

(h)   The cost of preprinted stationery

(i)   The cost of television advertising

(j)   The cost of cones of thread

(k)   Road fund licences for vehicles

(l)   The canteen chef's wages

1.6   Suggest likely cost centres or profit centres for each of the following:

A theatre in a provincial town, where touring productions are staged. The theatre has a bar and a confectionery counter. Ticket sales are dealt with by the theatre's own box office, and the plays are advertised locally.

A garage, which sells both new and used cars of two different makes. Cars are also repaired, serviced and valeted.

1.7 You work for Gold and Partners, Chartered Accountants, who have three offices in neighbouring districts in the suburbs of London. The Senior Partner, Lawrence Gold, sent the following memo to your line manager, Marie McCall. You have been asked to extract and prepare the information requested in the memo. The offices are referred to as R, S and T. They are all of similar size.

MEMORANDUM

To: M. McCall

From: L. Gold

Date: 26 October 20XX

Subject: Annual Review: year ended 30 September

I am in the process of reviewing the firm's figures for the year ended 30 September and require the following:

- Income totals for each of the three offices.

- Costs for each of the three offices, broken down into materials, labour and expenses.

- Profit and Return on Investment calculated for each office separately.

Please supply these as soon as possible.

You extract the following information from the records:

Income for the year ended 30 September:
Office R: £950,000
Office S: £869,000
Office T: £1,195,500

Materials costs for the year ended 30 September:
Office R: £75,000
Office S: £7,000
Office T: £8,400

Labour costs for the year ended 30 September:
Office R: £650,000
Office S: £550,000
Office T: £730,000

Expenses for the year ended 30 September:
Office R: £82,500
Office S: £69,000
Office T: £89,100

The amount of money invested in each office at 30 September is as follows:
Office R: £750,000
Office S: £900,000
Office T: £1,150,000

Which of these amounts appears to be incorrect and should be queried with Marie McCall?

Marie McCall investigates your query and agrees that an error has been made. The correct figure is £7,500, which you should use. She suggests that you write out of all the above information in columns, with one column for the narrative and one for each Office (see the format below). When you have calculated the profit for each office and the return on investment, these can also be entered in the columns, in order to present the information clearly for Lawrence Gold.

	Office R (£)	Office S (£)	Office T (£)
Materials			
Labour			
Expenses			
TOTAL COSTS			
Income			
PROFIT			
Money invested			
Return on Investment (%)			

1.8 In your summer holiday, you are doing some voluntary work in the office of a charity. The charity raises money through Members' Subscriptions, Shops, Street Collections and Donations and a Christmas Mail Order Catalogue. Much of the work done for the charity is unpaid, but there is a certain amount of paid work in essential administration. There are also some costs of materials and expenses which are not donated. The Christmas Mail Order has costs similar to businesses. The chief administrator of the charity has asked you to draw up a table, as follows:

YEAR ENDED 31 December	Street Collections and Donations (£)	Shops (£)	Christmas Mail Order (£)	Members' Subscriptions (£)
Materials				
Labour				
Expenses				
TOTAL COSTS				
Income				
Surplus of Income over total costs (see Note 1)				
Surplus as a percentage of Income (Note 2)				

> Note 1: Surplus = Income – total costs, similar to profit for a business
>
> Note 2: To calculate the surplus as a percentage of income, the formula is:
>
> $$\frac{SURPLUS}{INCOME} \times 100\%$$

You are to extract the following information for the year from the records and complete the table.

Christmas Mail Order
Income from sales was £375,300.
Costs were: materials £260,000, labour £46,000, expenses £13,000

Street Collections and Donations
Income was £12,650.
Costs were: materials £2,500, labour £3,000, expenses £1,800

Shops
Income was £78,600.
Costs were: materials £8,300, labour £21,000, expenses £5,700

Members' Subscriptions
Income was £11,200
Costs were: Materials £900, labour £3,000, expenses £1,800

1.9   In your everyday life there are almost certainly a number of coding systems which you use, or systems which apply codes to you personally or to your household. For example, the system of Post Codes, which in the UK consist of combinations of letters and numbers. Some coding systems use numbers only and some letters only.

Identify at least *three* coding systems which you use or which are applied to you in your everyday life. State whether the codes are made up of letters or numbers or combinations of both. Provide examples of the codes used within each system.

1.10   The following is an extract from the coding reference manual for a company which processes sugar beet. The sugar which is produced is then packed for distribution.

Extract from list of cost centre codes:

Beet preparation	010
Processing	020
Packing	030
Administration	040
Quality control	050
Distribution	060

Extract from list of expenditure codes:

Sugar beet	1010
Stationery	1050
Machine operators' wages	2010
Supervisory wages	2040
Drivers' wages	2050
Heating and lighting	3020
Power for machinery	3030
Telephone	3040

Each item of expenditure is to be coded with the appropriate cost centre code, followed by the expenditure code, eg Distribution drivers' wages would be coded 060 2050.

Determine the codes for the following in this way (ignore VAT):

(a)   Wages paid to machine operators in the processing department

(b)   Cost of telephone calls made by the administration department

(c)   Cost of electricity used for heating the packing department

(d)   Cost of stationery used in the administration department

(e)   Wages of the supervisor in the preparation department

(f)   Cost of a consignment of beet to be charged to the preparation department

(g)   Cost of power used to run the processing machines

(h)   Cost of stationery used by the quality control inspectors

14

2 FINANCIAL ACCOUNTING – FINANCIAL STATEMENTS

important note to students
As noted in the Tutorial text, this chapter is optional. The activities set out here will help you in your studies but will not be assessed in your Simulation. If in doubt, consult your tutor.

2.1   You have been asked to draft the Profit & Loss Account and Balance Sheet of Jack Daniels for the financial year ended 31 December. You have been given the proforma statements shown below and on the next page and are told to fill in the gaps with the correct figures. The figures you have been given are (in £):

Sales	300,000	Cost of Sales	160,000	Office expenses	10,500
Wages	40,100	Rent paid	8,750	Telephone	800
Premises	400,000	Computers	80,000	Stock	20,000
Debtors	25,500	Bank balance	850	Creditors	21,500
Opening capital	453,000	Drawings	28,000		

Profit and loss account
of Jack Daniels for the year ended 31 December

	£	£
Sales		300,000
Cost of Sales		160,000
Gross profit		140,000
Less overheads:		
Office expenses	10,500	
Wages	40,100	
Rent paid	8,750	
Telephone	800	
		60,150
Net profit		79,850

Balance sheet of Jack Daniels as at 31 December

	£	£
Fixed assets		
Premises		400,000
Computer equipment		80,000
		480,000
Current assets		
Stock	10,000	
Debtors	25,500	
Bank	850	
	46,350	
Less Current liabilities		
Creditors	21,500	
Working capital		24,850
NET ASSETS		504,850
FINANCED BY		
Capital		
Opening capital		453,000
Add net profit (from profit & loss account)		552,850
Less drawings		28,000
		504,850

2.2   When you have completed the forms, check your work carefully, ensuring that the balance sheet 'balances'.

Then set out the following figures, explaining what they mean:

(a)   gross profit

(b)   net profit

(c)   net assets

(d)   capital

3 MEASURING PERFORMANCE

3.1 Walton plc: Departmental monthly wages

Walton plc has five departments, A, B, C, D and E. The monthly wages for each of the departments are as follows:

A	B	C	D	E	Total
£24,500	£30,625	£15,925	£36,750	£14,700	£122,500

You are to:

(a) Calculate, for each department, the monthly cost of wages as a percentage of the total monthly wages of Walton plc.

(b) Calculate the new monthly wages for each department and the total for the company if departments A, B and C are given a 4% wage increase and departments D and E are given a 2% wage increase.

(c) Calculate the percentage increase in the total monthly wages for Walton plc that would result from the wage increases described in part (b).

3.2 Clover Cars has several branches and a total of 10 people selling cars. The following data relates to the weekly sales of cars over a 12-week period.

Clover Cars weekly sales

Week	1	2	3	4	5	6
Number of cars sold	20	18	20	24	25	28

Week	7	8	9	10	11	12
Number of cars sold	30	30	26	22	20	22

The expected average number of cars to be sold is 30 per week.

You are to calculate:

(a) the weekly labour productivity (output per employee)

(b) the weekly efficiency percentage (to the nearest %)

(c) the labour productivity and the efficiency percentage for the whole twelve-week period.

Set out your calculations on a spreadsheet or table. Comment briefly on the results, if possible using a word processing program.

3.3 Lite Luggage Limited is a manufacturer of luggage for air travel. The company sells its product to wholesalers. During the year it records the following figures for units made and sold and total production cost of units made and sold.

Lite Luggage Limited monthly production

	Units made and sold	Production costs
	(thousands)	(£000s)
January	40	740
February	35	728
March	30	720
April	40	760
May	32	704
June	36	720
July	40	780
August	35	735
September	32	720
October	30	690
November	36	738
December	40	760

You are to calculate:

(a) the production cost per unit in each month (to the nearest penny)

(b) the total units made and sold, total production cost and cost per unit for the first six months, January to June

(c) the total units made and sold, total production cost and cost per unit for the second six months, July to December

Set out the data and your answers on a spreadsheet or in a table and comment briefly on the results.

3.4 This activity uses some of the data and answers relating to Lite Luggage Limited from 3.3 above, together with additional information given below.

Lite Luggage Limited sells its product at £28 per unit in the first half of the year and £30 per unit in the second half of the year.

The overheads and capital employed during the year are as shown in the table.

You are to complete the table below or continue with your spreadsheet from 3.3 and:

(a)   use your answers to 3.3, parts (b) and (c), to calculate the Sales Revenue for the six months January to June and the six months July to December

(b)   enter the total production cost of units made and sold for each six-month period

(c)   calculate the gross profit and the net profit for each six-month period as shown in the table below

(d)   calculate the gross profit percentage and the net profit percentage for each six-month period (to the nearest %)

(e)   calculate the capital productivity and return on capital employed for each six-month period

(f)   complete the 'total for year' column as shown on the table below

(g)   comment briefly on the results of your calculations.

Lite Luggage Limited	January-June	July-December	Total for year
Units made and sold (000s)			
Selling price	£28 per unit	£30 per unit	
	£000s	£000s	£000s
Sales Revenue			
Production cost of units made and sold			
Gross Profit			
Overheads	600	620	1,220
Net Profit			
Gross Profit %			
Net Profit %			
Capital Employed (£000s)	3,500	3,500	3,500
Capital productivity (sales revenue per £1 of capital employed)			
Return on Capital Employed			

3.5   Daisy's Direct is a mail order gift service and has 4 employees working in the packing department. These employees normally work 38 hours per week. During a period of 8 weeks, the following hours were recorded by the 4 employees.

Daisy's Direct Packing Department: weekly hours								
Week:	1	2	3	4	5	6	7	8
Employee	**Hours per week**							
P Leigh	36	42	36	30	32	30	36	38
A Patel	36	40	35	36	32	32	38	38
R Napier	36	41	35	35	32	30	36	38
D Davis	36	43	36	38	30	32	36	38

You are to:

(a) Calculate the total hours worked in each week and the total hours worked by each employee in the 8-week period.

(b) Calculate the labour (resource) utilisation percentage for each week and for the whole 8-week period (to the nearest %).

(c) Comment briefly on the results.

3.6 The following figures were recorded by Unicreme Ice Cream Ltd for the four quarters of Year 2.

Production figures for Unicreme Ice Cream Ltd: Year 2				
Quarter	1	2	3	4
Units produced and sold	30,000	96,000	120,000	48,000
Expected output (units)	22,000	88,000	124,000	42,000
Sales (£)	60,000	175,000	215,000	95,000
Cost of production (£)	41,000	81,600	96,000	50,000
Hours worked	500	1,000	1,200	600

You are to calculate for each quarter:

(a) labour productivity (sales (£) per hour worked)

(b) units produced per hour worked

(c) efficiency percentage

(d) cost of production per unit

3.7 This activity uses some of the same data relating to Unicreme Ice Cream Ltd as in activity 3.6 above. The data required is repeated in the table below, together with additional figures for quarterly overheads.

Production figures for Unicreme Ice Cream Ltd: Year 2

Quarter	1	2	3	4	Total
	£	£	£	£	
Sales	60,000	175,000	215,000	95,000	
Cost of production	41,000	81,600	96,000	50,000	
Gross Profit					
Overheads	30,000	50,000	50,000	30,000	160,000
Net profit/(loss)					
Gross profit margin					
Net profit margin					

You are to:

(a) fill in the blank rows and columns in the table either manually or using a spreadsheet

(b) given that the capital employed by Unicreme in year 2 was £400,000, calculate for Year 2:

   (i) the capital productivity (sales per £1 of capital employed)

   (ii) the Return on Capital Employed

3.8 Davis Limited manufactures a fibre-glass product that requires the material to be cut and moulded before the product is finished and packed. The following budgeted and actual data relates to the four departments of Davis Ltd for a given year.

Davis Ltd Production and Labour Data for the year

Department	Cutting	Moulding	Finishing	Packing
Budgeted output (units)	200,000	200,000	180,000	180,000
Labour hours available	20,000	25,000	24,000	12,000
Actual output (units)	198,000	195,000	175,000	175,000
Actual labour hours worked	19,600	24,500	23,500	12,000
Actual cost of labour (£)	138,600	156,000	157,500	70,000
Average number of employees	11	14	13	7

You are to:

Set up the data on a spreadsheet or table and calculate the following performance indicators for each department of Davis Ltd:

(a) labour productivity as actual units of output per employee

(b) efficiency percentage comparing actual output with budgeted output

(c) labour utilisation percentage comparing actual hours with available hours

(d) actual cost of labour per unit of actual output

(e) for one of the performance indicators calculated, suggest a reason why comparison between the departments of Davis Ltd may be unfair to the employees.

3.9 You are an accounting technician employed by Mixed Retailers plc, which owns a large number of stores selling a wide variety of products throughout the UK. Mixed Retailers plc is currently investigating the performance of a number of companies retailing electrical goods with a view to purchasing a chain of stores in that sector of the market.

As an accounting technician in the accounting department of Mixed Retailers plc you have been asked by the chief accountant to carry out a number of analyses of the accounts of two companies retailing electrical goods.

You are to:

(a) Look at the following data for two years for two companies – Alpha and Beta – see the next page.

Analyse the data by completing the table on the next page.

Show the average size of store and sales per employee to the nearest whole number.

Show net profit/sales as a percentage to two decimal places.

(b) Prepare a report for the chief accountant comparing the performance of Alpha and Beta.

Your report should be well-presented and address the following issues:

• size

• profitability

• efficiency

Your report should conclude by presenting the key differences in performance between the two companies. You should not attempt to make recommendations.

PERFORMANCE DATA

Year	Company Alpha		Company Beta	
	Year 1	Year 2	Year 1	Year 2
Number of stores	281	279	226	231
Total area (sq m)	1,110,000	1,200,000	191,000	180,000
Number of employees	14,700	16,200	5,050	5,100
Sales (£m)	1,050	1,350	495	510
Net profit (£m)	51.1	52.0	15.7	16.8
Sales per sq m (£)	946	1,125	2,592	2,833
Average size of store (sq m)				
Net profit/sales (%)				
Sales per employee (£)				

3.10 You are an accounting technician working for City Hotels Limited, which owns three hotels in London.

- The Station Hotel is situated near a main railway station and its customers are mainly railway travellers, business people and weekend visitors.

- The Airport Hotel is situated near the airport and its customers are virtually all air travellers who stay in the hotel either before or after their flight.

- The Central Hotel is situated in the city centre and is used mainly by tourists, business people and weekend visitors.

City Hotels Limited wishes to compare the performances of the three hotels and has asked you to carry out a series of analyses to enable this to be done.

Basic Data

	Station Hotel	Airport Hotel	Central Hotel
Number of Rooms	140	210	90
Standard Room Tariff	£84.00	£90.00	£120.00

Notes:

- Each hotel has only double rooms. The standard room tariff is the price of a double room per night.
- City Hotels Limited runs a variety of discount schemes and special offers whereby rooms can be obtained at cheaper rates.

City Hotels Limited

Performance Statistics for the week ended 31 May

	Sun	Mon	Tues	Wed	Thurs	Fri	Sat
Station Hotel:							
No. of Rooms Let	80	110	108	106	105	96	121
Total Room Revenue	£5,712	£8,632	£8,624	£8,648	£8,442	£7,228	£6,920
Room Occupancy Rate	57%	79%	77%	76%	75%	69%	86%
Average Rate per Room Let	£71.40	£78.47	£79.85	£81.58	£80.40	£75.29	£57.19
Airport Hotel:							
No. of Rooms Let	182	192	186	174	195	184	173
Total Room Revenue	£16,148	£16,920	£16,482	£15,084	£16,836	£15,680	£15,036
Room Occupancy Rate	87%	91%	89%	83%	93%	88%	82%
Average Rate per Room Let	£88.73	£88.13	£88.61	£86.69	£86.34	£85.22	£86.91
Central Hotel:							
No. of Rooms Let	64	68	69	46	52	65	82
Total Room Revenue	£6,880	£7,304	£7,082	£4,832	£5,734	£6,432	£7,924
Room Occupancy Rate	71%	76%	77%	51%	58%	72%	91%
Average Rate per Room Let	£107.50	£107.41	£102.64	£105.04	£110.27	£98.95	£96.63

You are to:

(a)   Complete the Summary Performance Statistics (see the next page) for City Hotels Limited.

City Hotels Limited

Summary Performance Statistics for the week ended 31 May

	Station Hotel	Airport Hotel	Central Hotel
Total Rooms Let			
Average Room Occupancy Rate			
Total Room Revenue			
Average Rate per Room Let			

Note: Average room occupancy rate is to be shown to the nearest whole percentage. The average rate per room let is to be shown to the nearest penny.

(b)   Prepare a report for City Hotels Limited, comparing the performances of the three hotels for the week ending 31 May. Use the information given, together with the statistics prepared by you in part (a).

Your report could examine areas such as the following:

• room occupancy rates

• rates per room let

4 CHARTS, AVERAGES AND INDICES

4.1 Kaye Limited

You work for Kaye Limited, a company which has branches in three regions: North, Midlands and South. You have collected together sales revenue figures for the first six months of the year, January to June, for each of the company's three regions. The figures are given in thousands of pounds and are as follows (in date order):

North: 270, 310, 330, 320, 300, 290

Midlands: 350, 360, 375, 375, 380, 385

South: 180, 185, 200, 220, 240, 250

You are to:

Set out the above data in a table or on a spreadsheet, including totals for each month and totals for each region for the 6 months January to June.

4.2 Kaye Limited

Using the table or spreadsheet of data prepared in activity 4.1, construct the following diagrams to illustrate Kaye Limited's regional figures. For each diagram, comment briefly on what it does and does not show.

(a)   line graph

(b)   compound bar chart

(c)   component bar chart

(d)   pie chart, using the six-monthly totals only

You may construct the diagrams either manually or using a computer.

4.3   Clover Cars have several branches and a total of 10 people selling cars. The following data relates to the sales made by each of the 10 people over a 12-week period.

	Clover Cars Sales Analysis									
Sales person:	A	B	C	D	E	F	G	H	I	J
Number of cars sold:	18	31	24	28	22	31	35	38	31	27
Sales value of cars sold (£000s)	350	310	250	260	390	300	390	440	390	350

You are to:

(a)   Calculate the total number of cars sold in the period

(b)   Calculate the total sales value of cars sold in the period

(c)   Using your answers to (a) and (b), calculate:

   (i)   the mean number of cars sold per sales person
   (ii)   the mean value of cars sold per sales person
   (iii)   the mean value per car of all the cars sold in the period

(d)   Sort each set of data into size order and hence identify the median and the mode of each set.

(e)   Construct a simple bar chart to show the value of the cars sold by each of the sales staff.

You may carry out the activities either manually or using a computer.

4.4 Monthly Sales Revenue figures (in £000s) are shown below for the South region of Kaye Limited for a given year.

Kaye Ltd South Region monthly sales (£000s)			
January	180	July	256
February	185	August	268
March	200	September	280
April	220	October	285
May	240	November	306
June	250	December	313

You are to:

(a)   Construct a table showing the monthly sales revenue in a single column and calculate a 3-point moving average trend.

(b)   Calculate the average monthly increment in the trend (to the nearest whole number in £000s)

(c)   Use your answer to (b) to forecast the trend in monthly sales revenue for January and February of the next year

(d)   Construct a graph showing the original data and your forecasts of the trend for January and February of the next year.

4.5 The following table shows the sales and net profit figures for Broom Estate Agents for the last five years, together with the Retail Prices Index for those years.

Broom Estate Agents: sales and net profit for years 1 to 5			
	Sales	*Net Profit*	*RPI*
	£000s	*£000s*	
Year 1	800	120	155
Year 2	890	130	163
Year 3	920	140	169
Year 4	950	150	176
Year 5	990	160	189

You are to:

(a) Convert the sales and net profit figures into index numbers, using year 1 as a base

(b) Adjust the sales and net profit figures for the changing price levels shown by the Retail Prices Index. Put the figures into year 5 terms and give your answers to the nearest whole number.

(c) Comment briefly on the trends shown in your answers to (a) and (b) above.

4.6 You are an accounting technician employed by Mixed Retailers plc, which owns a large number of stores selling a wide variety of products throughout the UK. Mixed Retailers plc is currently investigating the performance of a number of companies retailing electrical goods with a view to purchasing a chain of stores in that sector of the market.

Mixed Retailers plc is thinking of purchasing Company Gamma. The chief accountant of Mixed Retailers plc is concerned about some comments made in the annual report of Gamma. In this report the managing director of Gamma makes the following statement:

'Although sales have increased each year over the last five years, net profit took a slight dip in Years 3 and 4 before rising to a record level in Year 5.'

Relevant figures from the report are as follows:

	Year 1	Year 2	Year 3	Year 4	Year 5
Sales (£m)	3003.6	3235.4	3288.8	3547.9	4479.4
Net profit (£m)	237.6	240.5	218.9	208.7	318.2
% Change in Net Profit	–	1.22%	- 8.98%	- 4.66%	52.47%	
Net profit as % of sales	7.91%	7.43%	6.66%	5.88%	7.10%
Sales at Year 5 prices (£m)					
Net profit at Year 5 prices (£m)	269.5	264.1	231.1	214.2	318.2
Trade Price Index	133.3	137.7	143.2	147.3	151.2

You are to:

(a) Complete the table above by calculating sales for each year at Year 5 prices using the Trade Price Index. Your figures should be shown as £m rounded to one decimal place.

(b) Prepare a line graph, showing the trend in sales and net profit at Year 5 prices from Year 1 to Year 5.

(c) Write a memo, stating whether you agree or disagree with the statement made by the managing director of Gamma. Support your conclusions with evidence, using the data given and your answers to (a) and (b).

4.7 You are an accounting technician working for City Hotels Limited, which owns three hotels in London.

- The Station Hotel is situated near a main railway station and its customers are mainly railway travellers, business people and weekend visitors.

- The Airport Hotel is situated near the airport and its customers are virtually all air travellers who stay in the hotel either before or after their flight.

- The Central Hotel is situated in the city centre and is used mainly by tourists, business people and weekend visitors.

City Hotels Limited wishes to compare the performances of the three hotels and has asked you to compare the revenue from rooms let for the three hotels over the last five years.

City Hotels Limited

Revenue from Rooms Let: Years 1 - 5

	Year 1	Year 2	Year 3	Year 4	Year 5
Station Hotel	£2,300,000	£2,500,000	£2,400,000	£2,500,000	£2,600,000
Airport Hotel	£2,500,000	£2,800,000	£4,600,000	£5,200,000	£5,500,000
Central Hotel	£1,700,000	£1,800,000	£1,700,000	£1,900,000	£2,200,000

You are to:

(a) Prepare a clearly labelled line graph showing the performance of the three hotels for the five year period.

(b) Prepare a memorandum for the hotel accountant. The memorandum should note the trends revealed by the graph prepared in part (a) and suggest any problems associated with relying on the figures in the table as they stand.

5 REPORT WRITING

5.1 BCL Ltd specialises in the manufacture of computer hardware and software and the provision of computer consultancy services. In recent years, the software and consultancy business has expanded.

BCL Ltd sells hardware to both commercial and government organisations. The commercial hardware market is becoming more competitive and development costs are rising. The government hardware business is currently restricted by government spending limits, but is expected to improve in the long term. Government hardware contracts often provide additional work for the software and consultancy division of BCL Ltd.

You work in the finance department of BCL Ltd and have been given the following data for Years 1 and 2, relating to the three divisions of the company: Commercial Hardware, Government Hardware and Software and Consultancy.

The performance figures given in bold type for Year 2 have been prepared by a trainee. They are shown on the next page. The trainee is rather inexperienced and says that there may be some errors in his calculations.

You are to:

Correct and rewrite (or prepare using a spreadsheet) the table of performance indicators for BCL Ltd for the years shown.

BCL LTD DATA FOR YEAR 2

	Commercial Hardware	Government Hardware	Software and Consultancy
	£000s	£000s	£000s
Sales revenue	15,957	24,768	11,368
Development costs	6,376	7,832	2,134
Other costs	7,215	8,150	3,716
Net profit	2,366	8,786	5,518
Number of employees	831	607	423

BCL LTD PERFORMANCE INDICATORS FOR YEARS 1 & 2

	Year 1	Year 2
Commercial Hardware		
Sales revenue (£000s)	17,643	15,957
Net profit margin	17.5%	**12.1%**
Development costs as a percentage of sales	34.7%	**40.0%**
Sales per employee (£)	22,107	**19,202**
Government Hardware		
Sales revenue (£000s)	25,974	24,768
Net profit margin	36.6%	**35.5%**
Development costs as a percentage of sales	30.9%	**31.6%**
Sales per employee (£)	41,200	**40,408**
Software and Consultancy		
Sales revenue (£000s)	9,276	11,368
Net profit margin	39.4%	**48.5%**
Development costs as a percentage of sales	21.7%	**18.3%**
Sales per employee (£)	23,614	**26,875**

5.2 Rainbow plc is a paint manufacturer and the information below relates to Rainbow plc for Year 2.

Rainbow plc

Summary Profit and Loss Account for the year ended 30 June (Year 2)

	£000s	£000s
Sales		3,500
Less: Cost of Sales		1,590
Gross Profit		1,910
Administration	780	
Selling and Distribution	505	
		1,285
Net Profit		625
Capital employed		2,840

You are to:

(a) Calculate the following ratios for Rainbow plc for Year 2:

Gross profit as a percentage of sales

Net profit as a percentage of sales

Return on Capital Employed (ROCE)

Capital productivity as Sales (£)/Capital employed

(b) Given the following comparative data for Rainbow plc for the previous financial year, write brief comments on the company's performance over the two years.

Rainbow plc Performance data for the year ended 30 June (Year 1)

Gross profit as a percentage of sales	52%
Net profit as a percentage of sales	21%
Return on Capital Employed	24%
Capital productivity	£1.16

5.3 The Wichenford Bus Company runs regular bus services on two main routes and the managers of the company wish to compare the profitability of these routes over the last six month period. You are given the following information for the two routes for the given period:

Bus services data for 6 months

	Route A	Route B
Number of vehicles used	6	8
Total mileage for 6 months	35,000 miles	47,000 miles
Sales Revenue	£157,500	£169,200
Total costs	£148,000	£156,700

You are to:

(a) Set up the data on a table or spreadsheet and calculate for the given period for each route:

- average sales revenue per mile
- total cost per mile
- average mileage per vehicle
- net profit
- net profit as a percentage of sales revenue
- net profit per mile

(b) Prepare a short report for the management of the Wichenford Bus Company, commenting on the results for routes A and B for the given period. Include in your report a compound bar chart to show how the two routes compare for sales revenue per mile, total cost per mile and net profit per mile.

5.4 Bradshaw plc runs two chains of shops selling electrical goods, under the names Brad and Shaw. The Brad chain of shops offers lower prices but a smaller range of goods than the Shaw chain.

The data below relates to the two chains of shops for Year 1 and Year 2

Bradshaw plc Data for the years ended 30 September:

	Year 1		Year 2	
	Brad	*Shaw*	*Brad*	*Shaw*
Sales (£000s)	33,000	58,000	36,000	55,000
Net profit (£000s)	6,000	10,000	6,000	11,000
Number of shops	9	14	10	11
Total area in square metres	17,100	39,000	20,000	32,000
Number of employees	630	850	750	680

You are to:

(a) Set up the data on a table or spreadsheet and calculate for each chain for each year:
- the average area in square metres per shop
- the sales revenue per square metre
- the sales revenue per employee
- the net profit as a percentage of sales

(b) Prepare some notes for the management of Bradshaw plc commenting on the performance of the two chains of shops over the given two year period.

6 CONSOLIDATING AND REPORTING INFORMATION

6.1 Sam runs a restaurant and a separate catering service for functions. The data given below relates to the 3 months April to June of Year 2, together with comparative data for the same period in Year 1. Sam has asked you to consolidate the figures for the two parts of the business and report back with your comments, but he asked why you wanted the data for April to June of Year 1, rather than just comparing April to June of Year 2 with the previous quarter, January to March of Year 2.

Sam's Restaurant and Catering Services April-June (Year 2)			
	Restaurant £	Catering Services £	Total £
Sales	145,000	95,000	
Cost of Sales	85,000	57,000	
Gross Profit	60,000	38,000	
Overheads	39,000	20,000	
Net Profit	21,000	18,000	
Gross Profit margin			
Net Profit margin			
Percentage increases in sales compared to the same period in Year 1:			
Sales increase			

Sam's Restaurant and Catering Services April-June (Year 1)			
	Restaurant £	Catering Services £	Total £
Sales	130,000	80,000	
Cost of Sales	70,000	50,000	
Gross Profit	60,000	30,000	
Overheads	40,000	15,000	
Net Profit	20,000	15,000	
Gross Profit margin			
Net Profit margin			

You are to:

(a) Set up the data on a spreadsheet and complete the total columns, profit margin percentages and percentage increases in sales using formulas. Alternatively, calculate the required figures and enter them in the tables.

(b) Write brief comments on the sales and profitability of the business and suggest an answer for Sam's question.

6.2 Elmwood Retailers Limited owns three shops selling fashion accessories. Branches P and Q are of similar size. Branch R is a smaller shop. You are given the following table of data to complete for Elmwood Retailers Ltd. Note that no adjustments are needed to the sales or purchases figures for the transfers of stock between the branches.

Note also that the Cost of Sales figure is calculated by *adding* Opening Stock to Purchases and then *deducting* Closing Stock.

Elmwood Retailers Ltd

Summary Profit and Loss Account for the year ended 30 June

	Branch P £000s	Branch Q £000s	Branch R £000s	Total £000s
Sales	700	900	300	
Opening stock	70	70	40	
Purchases	440	630	200	
Less: Closing stock	60	120	40	
Cost of sales				
Gross profit				
Overheads	160	180	60	
Net profit				
Transfers	(30)	20	10	
Gross profit %				
Net profit %				

You are to:

(a) Complete the table using a spreadsheet if possible.

(b) Prepare a short report for the managers of Elmwood Retailers Ltd, explaining briefly the main points shown by the completed table.

6.3 Greenpark Limited has two large golf equipment shops, Green and Park. The following data relates to the week ended 30 June.

On 29 June £5,000 of stock was sent from Green to Park, but this was not recorded in the books of Park until 2 July.

GREENPARK LIMITED

RESULTS FOR THE WEEK ENDED 30 JUNE

	Green		Park		Total	
	£000s	£000s	£000s	£000s	£000s	£000s
Sales		85		60		
Opening stock	10		9			
Purchases	40		35			
Less: Closing stock	10		15			
Cost of goods sold		____		____		____
Gross profit						
Overheads		30		20		____
Net profit						
		____		____		____
Transfers		(5)				
Gross profit %						
Net profit %						

You are to:

(a) Complete the table, using a spreadsheet if possible. Make the appropriate adjustment for stock in transit. (No adjustment need be made to sales or purchases figures.)

(b) Write a memo to the managing director of Greenpark Ltd, commenting briefly on the results for the week ended 30 June.

6.4 Dale Hotels Ltd owns a chain of hotels and divides the country into four regions for administrative purposes: South-East, South-West, Midlands and North. The company measures the available capacity of the hotels in terms of the number of guest-days, for example: a hotel with enough space for 100 guests and which is open for 365 days a year would have 100 x 365 = 36,500 guest-days available for the year.

The actual usage of the hotels is measured in customer-days. A comparison of customer-days with the total available guest-days shows how well the hotels have been used during a period.

You are a trainee accountant working in the head office of Dale Hotels Ltd and are given the following data and some tasks to complete. The financial year end for Dale Hotels is 31 December.

Dale Hotels Ltd: Data for the year ended 31 December Year 4						
Region	South-East	South-West	Midlands	North		Total
Number of hotels	4	4	4	3		
Available guest-days (000s)	140	135	130	100		
Actual customer-days (000s)						
Tourists	45	70	35	50		
Business	60	25	65	25		
Total	105	95	100	75		
Percentage used in the year	75%	70%	77%	75%		
	£000s	£000s	£000s	£000s		£000s
Sales revenue	5,400	5,600	5,200	4,800		
Total costs	4,590	4,900	4,430	4,150		
Net profit	810	700	770	650		
Average sales revenue per hotel						
Net profit %						
Average sales revenue per customer-day						

Dale Hotels Ltd Sales Revenue for Years 1 - 4			
Year	Total Sales Revenue £000s	Retail Prices Index	Adjusted Total Sales Revenue £000s
Year 1	19,400	172	
Year 2	20,300	173	
Year 3	20,800	178	
Year 4	21,000	184	

You are to:

(a)   Complete both the tables given above and on the previous page.

Give the net profit percentages correct to one decimal place.

In the second table, showing total sales revenue for the 4 years, the Retail Prices Index is to be used to adjust the sales revenue figures to Year 4 terms.

(b)   Prepare comments on the data in both completed tables for the management of Dale Hotels Ltd, covering:

- profitability of the various regions
- the difference made to sales revenue by adjusting for the Retail Prices Index

6.5 Enigma Electronics Limited makes 'Nimrod' satellite navigation systems for car manufacturers in its factory in Mereford, West Midlands, UK. The company is organised in three divisions:

Manufacturing Division manufactures the component parts of the navigation systems.

Assembly Division puts together the systems in a variety of configurations according to the specifications of the various car manufacturers who order them.

Administration Division organises the marketing and sales of the systems and also provides the other support functions of the company.

At the end of the financial year you are given the summary cost statements for the Manufacturing and Assembly Divisions and the cost and revenue statement of the Administration Division.

You are to consolidate the data from these three statements on the spreadsheet format on the next page. You may set up the spreadsheet if you wish. You should note that all transfers between divisions are at cost and the effects of them should be removed when preparing the consolidated statement.

Cost Statement: Manufacturing Division

Year ended 31 December 2006

		£
	Opening stock of raw materials	60,500
add	Purchases of raw materials	490,000
		550,500
less	Closing stock of raw materials	71,000
	Total usage of raw materials	479,500
add	Factory labour costs	350,000
add	Factory overheads	275,000
	Transfer cost to Assembly Division	**1,104,500**

Cost Statement: Assembly Division

Year ended 31 December 2006

		£
	Opening stock of raw materials	52,000
add	Purchases of raw materials from external suppliers	255,700
add	**Transfer cost from Manufacturing Division**	**1,104,500**
		1,412,200
less	Closing stock of raw materials	85,900
	Total usage of raw materials	1,326,300
add	Factory labour costs	225,600
add	Factory overheads	226,300
	Transfer cost to Administration Division	**1,778,200**

Cost and Revenue Statement: Administration Division

Year ended 31 December 2006

		£	£
	Sales		3,376,800
	Cost of goods sold:		
	Opening cost of finished goods	148,200	
add	**Transfer cost from Assembly Division**	**1,778,200**	
		1,926,400	
less	Closing stock of finished goods	136,000	
	Total cost of goods sold	1,790,400	
add	Administration salaries	570,000	
add	Administration costs	653,000	
	Total costs		3,013,400
	Net profit		**363,400**

	A	B	C	D	E	F
1	Enigma Electronics Limited: Consolidated statement of cost and revenues					
2	Year ended 31 December 2006					
3						
4			Manufacturing Division	Assembly Division	Admin Division	Consolidated
5			£	£	£	£
6						
7		Sales				
8						
9		Cost of goods sold				
10		Opening stock of finished goods				
11	plus	Total usage of raw materials				
12	plus	Total factory labour				
13	plus	Total factory overheads				
14						
15	less	Closing stock of finished goods				
16		Total cost of goods sold				
17						
18		Gross profit				
19						
20	less	Administration salaries				
21	less	Administration costs				
22						
23		Net profit				
24						

6.6 This activity, together with Activities 6.7 and 6.8 continue the scenario introduced in Activity 6.5. You should check with your tutor that your calculations for Activity 6.5 are correct before proceeding any further.

You have been asked by the management of Enigma Electronics Limited to calculate performance indicators. They have asked you to work out for the financial year ending 31 December 2006:

(a) gross profit margin (to nearest %)

(b) net profit margin (to nearest %)

(c) return on capital employed (to nearest %)

(d) efficiency of production (to nearest %)

(e) labour productivity per employee (to nearest unit)

You are given the following data:

Capital employed for year ended 31 December 2006	£6 million
Target number of navigation systems for production in the year	90,000
Number of navigation systems produced in year ended 30 June 2006	85,400
Staff employed in the year ended 30 June 2006	320

They provide you with a proforma table on which to record the data. This is shown below.

ENIGMA ELECTRONICS LIMITED

Performance indicators for year ended 31 December 2006.

Gross profit margin	
Net profit margin	
Return on capital employed	
Efficiency of production	
Labour productivity	

6.7 This activity, together with Activities 6.6 and 6.8 continue the scenario introduced in Activity 6.5. You should check with your tutor – if you have not already done so – that your calculations for Activity 6.5 are correct before proceeding any further.

You have been asked to provide further management information in the form of a comparison of the company's costs and revenues for the last two financial years: 2005 and 2006.

Because of changing price levels, you will have to adjust (increase) the figures for 2005 by certain percentages so that a true comparison can be made with the figures for 2006. The changes over the year are:

- selling prices have risen by 3%
- raw materials costs have risen by 4%
- the cost of factory labour has risen by 2%
- factory overheads have risen by 5%
- sales and administration salaries have risen by 3%
- other sales and administration costs have risen by 4%

The data should be entered in the 'adjusted' column of the spreadsheet shown below. Note that the value of stock of finished goods should not be adjusted, but remain the same.

	A	B	C	D	E	F
1	Enigma Electronics Ltd: Consolidated Statement of Revenues and Costs					
2	Year ended 30 June 2005					
3						
4			Adjusted		Unadjusted	
5			£	£	£	£
6						
7		Sales				3,067,000
8						
9		Cost of goods sold				
10						
11		Opening stock of finished goods			140,000	
12	add	Total usage of raw materials			680,000	
13	add	Total factory labour			560,000	
14	add	Total factory overheads			495,000	
15					1,875,000	
16	less	Closing stock of finished goods			148,200	
17		Total cost of goods sold				1,726,800
18						
19		Gross profit				1,340,200
20						
21	less	Administration salaries			500,000	
22						
23	less:	Administration costs			610,000	
24						
25		Net profit before taxation				1,110,000
26						230,200

6.8   You have been asked to compare the adjusted 2005 figures with the 2006 results and enter them on the spreadsheet shown below. You need to work out the difference in the figures over the two years, both in money amounts and also in percentage terms.

You have also been asked to make brief comments on the performance of the business over the two years. Set out your comments in a word processed file; you could use a table for the figures and headings and bullet points for your comments as appropriate.

	A	B	C	D	E
1	**Enigma Electronics Ltd: Comparison of actual 2006 results with adjusted 2005 results**				
2					
3					
4		Actual 2006	Adjusted 2005	Difference	Difference
5		£	£	£	%
6					
7	Sales				
8					
9	Gross profit				
10					
11	Net profit				
12					
13	Factory labour costs				
14					
15	Administration salaries				
16					

7 PREPARING EXTERNAL REPORTS

7.1 Dale Hotels Ltd is planning to expand its chain of hotels and is seeking a long-term bank loan. An extract from the application form for the loan is given on the next page and you are asked to complete it.

For completion of the form, you will need to refer to activity 6.4 on page 39 and the answers for that activity. If you have not yet completed activity 6.4 you will need to do so now, or obtain the answers from your tutor. You will also need the following additional information about Dale Hotels Ltd:

- The net profit calculated in activity 6.4 is after all expenses and before taxation

- The total net profit for Dale Hotels Ltd for the year ended 31 December Year 3 was £2,790,000.

- The total gross profit for Dale Hotels Ltd for the year ended 31 December Year 4 was £7,875,000.

- The capital employed by Dale Hotels Ltd in the year ended 31 December Year 4 was £9,980,000.

LOAN APPLICATION (extract)

Name of applicant company _____

Latest year for which accounting information is available   _____

Total sales revenue

In latest year for which accounts are available   £ _____

In previous year   £ _____

Percentage change (+/-)   _____

Net profit after all expenses, before taxation

In latest year for which accounts are available   £ _____

In previous year   £ _____

Percentage change (+/-)   _____

Gross profit margin (%)   _____

Net profit margin (%)   _____

Return on capital employed (%)   _____

Notes

1. In the case of a company with a divisional structure, all figures should refer to the results of the company as a whole, not to individual divisions within the company.

2. Unless otherwise stated, all questions relate to the latest year for which accounting information is available.

3. Figures should be actual historical values, with no indexing for inflation.

4. Return on capital employed is defined as net profit for the year before taxation, divided by total capital employed.

5. Percentages are to be given correct to one decimal place.

7.2 This activity is independent of activities 6.4 and 7.1 above and relates to a single hotel in the Dale Hotels chain – the Skipton Dale Hotel, Devonshire Street, Skipton, North Yorkshire.

Each hotel in the chain is required to submit a quarterly return of statistics to the Regional Tourist Office. You are currently working as assistant manager at the Skipton Dale Hotel and the manager, Beth Lang, has given you some notes about the last quarter, January to March Year 5, during which the hotel was open for 90 days.

Notes from hotel manager:

For the 90 days the hotel was open in the quarter January to March, we had 52 rooms available, 45 of them double and the rest single. At that time of year we have more business customers than usual: business customer-days were 3,000 out of a total of 5,250 customer-days for the quarter, the rest being tourists.

You are to complete the Quarterly Return of Statistics, given on the next page, for the Skipton Dale Hotel for the quarter ended 31 March Year 5, using the manager's notes and other information given above.

NORTHERN TOURIST AUTHORITY

QUARTERLY RETURN OF STATISTICS

Quarter ended: _____

Name of Hotel: _____

Address:

Manager: _____

Number of rooms:

Double _____ Single _____ Total _____

Number of beds available (2 per double room plus one per single room): _____ (a)

Number of days hotel open this quarter: _____ (b)

Total guest-days available this quarter: (a) x (b) _____ (c)

Customer-days this quarter:

Tourists _____ Business _____ Total _____ (d)

Percentage occupancy: (d) as a percentage of (c) _____

Signed: _____ Date: _____

Job title: _____

7.3 Greenpark Ltd is a company that runs golf equipment shops. (This activity is independent of Activity 6.3. which also features Greenpark Ltd).

Greenpark Ltd financed expansion of one of its shops with a long-term loan from the bank. The company undertook to provide trading figures to the bank on a monthly basis, so that the bank may monitor its progress.

A 'Statement of Current Trading Position' is shown on the next page, with some of the figures entered as at 30 June for Greenpark Ltd.

You are given the following additional information relating to the company's Current Liabilities (short-term debts) as at 30 June:

- Greenpark Ltd owes a total of £152,000 to its trade suppliers, most of this having been outstanding for less than 30 days. Only £8,500 of the total has been outstanding for between 31 and 60 days and none has been outstanding for more than 60 days.

- Greenpark Ltd has no overdrawn bank balances. The company owes £1,300 PAYE to HM Revenue & Customs and £45,600 in VAT, also to HM Revenue & Customs. It has no other amounts owing at 30 June.

You are to complete the remaining sections of the Statement of Current Trading Position shown on the next page for Greenpark Ltd as at 30 June.

Statement of Current Trading Position
("Quick Figures")

Business Name	GREENPARK LIMITED
As at (date)	30 JUNE

Current Assets

a. Total Trade Debtors (ie. funds owed to you by your customers)   £   77,700

Please give a breakdown of your trade debtors according to how long they have been outstanding:

Up to 30 days	£	62,100
31 to 60 days	£	14,500
Over 60 days	£	1,100

b. Stock and Work in Progress   £   30,000

c. Cash Held and Total of all Bank and Building Society Credit Balances in your books   £   98,600

d. Other Current Assets (please specify, eg. prepayments)   PREPAYMENT: TELEPHONE RENTAL

    £   100

Total Current Assets   (a)+(b)+(c)+(d)   £   206,400

Current Liabilities

e. Trade Creditors (ie. funds you owe your suppliers)   £

Please give a breakdown of your trade creditors according to how long they have been outstanding:

Up to 30 days	£
31 to 60 days	£
Over 60 days	£

f. Total of all Overdrawn Bank Balances in your books   £

g. Pay As You Earn (PAYE) Owed by the Business   £

h. Value Added Tax (VAT) Owed by the Business   £

i. Other Current Liabilities (please specify, eg. accruals)

    £

Total Current Liabilities   (e)+(f)+(g)+(h)+(i)   £

8 BASIC PRINCIPLES OF VAT

8.1 You are working in the accounts office of a local manufacturing firm. You have been given a batch of invoices to prepare. Among them are five invoices for customers who are quoted a 5% cash discount for settlement within 7 days.

Calculate the VAT due (at the current rate) and the invoice total, using the following table:

invoice	net total (before VAT) £	VAT £	invoice total £
4563	1,265.75		
4567	456.25		
4571	5,678.90		
4575	45.60		
4578	415.50		

8.2 On the next three pages are examples of sales invoices issued by VAT registered businesses.

Are they valid VAT invoices? If not, why not?

SALES INVOICE

Keeping Sweet
Confectioners

29 Mintfield Street, Broadfield, BR7 4ER
Tel 01908 887634 Fax 01908 887239 Email sugarplum@sweet.goblin.com

Delia's Deli
36 The Arcade
Broadfield
BR1 4GH

invoice no	**893823**
account	**3945**
your reference	**SP84**
date/tax point	**21 04 06**

deliver to

as above

details	quantity	price	amount (excl VAT)	VAT rate %	VAT amount £
Cheesecake — summerfruit	20	5.50	110.00		19.25
Raspberry Pavlova	30	6.25	187.50		32.81

terms
Net monthly
Carriage paid
E & OE

Total (excl VAT)	297.50
VAT	52.06
TOTAL	349.56

SALES INVOICE

Trend Designs

Unit 40 Elgar Estate, Broadfield, BR7 4ER
Tel 01908 765365 Fax 01908 7659507 Email lisa@trend.u-net.com
VAT Reg GB 0745 4172 20

invoice to

'Tone Up' Sports Shop	
38 The Arcade	
Broadfield	
BR1 4GH	

invoice no	788776
account	4013
your reference	2067
date/tax point	21 05 06

deliver to

as above

details	quantity	price	amount (excl VAT)	VAT rate %	VAT amount £
'Surf Dood' T-shirts	20	5.50	110.00	17.5	19.25
'Surf Baby' tracksuits	15	15.50	232.50	17.5	40.69

terms
Net monthly
Carriage paid
E & OE

Total (excl VAT)	342.50
VAT	59.94
TOTAL	402.44

SALES INVOICE

Champ Cleaners
17 High Street, Broadfield, BR7 4ER
Tel 01908 283472 Fax 01908 283488

invoice to

Premier Insurance **49 Farrier Street** **Broadfield** **BR1 4LY**

invoice no	**787906**
account	**3993**
your reference	**1956**

details	price
Office Cleaning 16 hrs	**104.00**

Total (excl VAT)	
VAT	
TOTAL	**122.20**

8.3 You work in the accounts office of a building firm. A trainee working on Purchase Ledger brings to your attention a number of low value invoices received from T Walker Joinery (which is registered for VAT). These invoices do not have the VAT amount specified – just the overall total. They *do* show the name and address of the supplier, the VAT registration number, the date of supply, the details of the goods and the VAT rate. The amounts are:

1 £18.21

2 £64.62

3 £94.00

4 £1.76

5 £93.94

6 £23.50

The trainee says "These are not valid VAT invoices – how are we supposed to enter them in the day book? There is no VAT amount shown."

You are to:

(a) State whether the invoices are valid invoices, and if they are, why they are.

(b) Show the trainee how to work out the VAT and the net amount by carrying out the appropriate calculation for all six invoices.

9 VAT ACCOUNTING AND THE VAT RETURN

9.1 You work for Simpson & Co, Accountants, and have been given the VAT figures from the accounts of four clients.

You are to draw up a VAT control account for each client company to calculate the VAT due or reclaimable for the VAT period. You can use the format shown at the bottom of the page. If the final total is reclaimable VAT, it should be shown in brackets.

VAT FIGURES	Homer Ltd	Bart Ltd	Marge Ltd	Lisa Ltd
	£	£	£	£
Purchases Day Book	3,120.00	2,739.50	7,826.65	2,713.50
Sales Day Book	6,461.70	4,806.33	10,632.40	985.67
Credit notes received	530.50	231.60	987.60	156.70
Credit notes issued	245.79	542.77	876.34	87.23
Cash book purchases (non-credit)	567.90	765.91	145.78	978.67
Cash book sales (non-credit)	461.75	1,675.80	1,287.89	568.23
Petty cash book purchases	15.95	21.67	45.78	24.55
EU Acquisitions	796.30	nil	4,875.89	nil
VAT overpaid previous period	nil	345.78	654.89	78.60
VAT underpaid previous period	34.87	nil	637.98	nil
Bad debt relief	156.67	476.50	nil	65.50

VAT deductible (input tax)	VAT payable (output tax)
Purchases Day Book VAT total, *less* any credit notes received	Sales Day Book VAT total, *less* any sales credit notes issued
Cash Book – items not in Purchases Day Book	Cash Book – items not in Sales Day Book
Petty Cash Book – VAT on small expenses	
Acquisitions from EU states	Acquisitions from EU states
Corrections of errors from previous periods (not exceeding £2,000 net)	Corrections of errors from previous periods (not exceeding £2,000 net)
Bad debt relief	
= TOTAL TAX DEDUCTIBLE	= TOTAL TAX PAYABLE
	less TOTAL TAX DEDUCTIBLE
	equals TAX PAYABLE/(RECLAIMABLE)

9.2   In your work for Simpson & Co you have been asked to sort out the VAT Return of Damon Driver, a local businessman who has set up a computer equipment firm in the town. He has presented you with two box files of invoices, one marked 'Purchases/expenses' and the other marked 'Sales'. He says he has been 'so busy' that he hasn't had time to sort them out. You make a list of the invoices as follows:

PURCHASES/EXPENSES				SALES			
Supplier	net £	VAT £	gross £	Customer	net £	VAT £	gross £
Amax Machines	234.56	41.04	275.60	B Keaton	56.00	9.80	65.80
Electra Limited	5,467.80	956.86	6,424.66	C Chaplin	678.00	118.65	796.65
Microhard PLC	9,567.90	1,674.38	11,242.28	Laurel College	45,786.90	8,012.70	53,799.60
Peach Computers	5,278.89	923.80	6,202.69	Hardy & Co	17,678.50	3,093.73	20,772.23
Elsa Products	560.00	98.00	658.00	A Sim	1,250.00	218.75	1,468.75
IPM Computers	19,780.00	3,461.50	23,241.50	T Thomas	16,900.00	2,957.50	19,857.50
				E Sykes Ltd	12,500.00	2,187.50	14,687.50
				H Jacques	3,467.80	606.86	4,074.66
				V Singh	450.00	78.75	528.75
				L San	400.00	70.00	470.00
				A Larsen	125.00	21.87	146.87
				Z Zidane	780.50	136.58	917.08
				M Santos	56.00	9.80	65.80

Damon tells you that these are all the credit transactions for the quarter. He also mentions:
* he has made cash sales of £940 (including VAT) and incurred petty cash expenses of £76.37 (including VAT)
* there were no EU acquisitions, corrections, bad debts, or credit notes issued or received

You are to:

(a)   total the money columns of the invoice listings in the above table

(b)   construct a VAT control account (see the previous page for the format)

(c)   state what figures you would transfer to the VAT 100 by completing the schedule below

VAT due on sales and other outputs	
VAT reclaimed on purchases	
VAT due/reclaimable	
Total value of sales and other outputs (excluding VAT)	
Total value of purchases and other inputs (excluding VAT)	

9.3 Julie Roberts is managing director of Pretty Woman Limited, a company which manufactures cosmetic accessories. The business is VAT-registered and submits its VAT Return quarterly at the end of March, June, September and December.

The business address is Unit 17 Everbeech Estate, Newtown, NW3 5TG. The VAT Registration number is 454 7106 51.

You work in the accounts department of Pretty Woman Limited and have been given the task of completing the VAT Return for the quarter ending 31 December of the current year.

You have collected the following data from the manual accounting records.

SALES DAY BOOK SUMMARY	standard-rated sales	VAT	total sales
	£	£	£
October	2,567.89	449.38	3,017.27
November	2,675.90	468.28	3,144.18
December	3,456.89	604.95	4,061.84

PURCHASES DAY BOOK SUMMARY	standard-rated purchases	VAT	total purchases
	£	£	£
October	1,456.90	254.95	1,711.85
November	3,456.20	604.83	4,061.03
December	1,490.25	260.79	1,751.04

CASH BOOK & PETTY CASH BOOK – NON CREDIT ITEMS (October - December)	net	VAT	total
	£	£	£
Cash sales	1,245.67	217.99	1,463.66
Petty cash expenses	67.80	11.86	79.66

ADDITIONAL INFORMATION

- Acquisitions from the EU for the period amounted to £850.70 net (VAT due of £148.87).

- Sales credit notes issued during the quarter amount to £345.70 + £60.49 VAT = £406.19.

- Credit notes received from suppliers amount to £400.00 + £70.00 VAT = £470.00.

- Bad debts written off during the year are:

    - £528.75 (invoice due 15 March, goods supplied 14 February)

    - £693.21 (invoice due 20 August, goods supplied 20 July)

    These invoice totals include VAT.

- In the previous VAT quarter there were two small errors in the accounts: output (sales) tax was underpaid by £44.50 and input tax (purchases) was over-estimated by £55.50.

You are to:

(a)   Complete the VAT Control Account (format shown below) for the October - December quarter.

(b)   Complete the VAT 100 form shown on the next page, ready for Julie Roberts' signature. Note that the year is shown as 'XX'; in reality the year would be shown as two digits.

VAT control account			
VAT deductible: input tax		**VAT payable: output tax**	
	£		£
Purchases Day Book		Sales Day Book	
less credit notes		*less* credit notes	
Cash Book		Cash Book	
Petty Cash Book			
EU Acquisitions		EU Acquisitions	
Correction of error		Correction of error	
Bad debt relief			
TOTAL INPUT TAX		TOTAL OUTPUT TAX	
		less TOTAL INPUT TAX	
		equals VAT DUE	

SPECIMEN

HM Customs and Excise

For the period
01 10 XX to 31 12 XX

625 454 7108 51 100 03 99 Q25147

PRETTY WOMAN LIMITED
17 EVERBEECH ESTATE
NEWTOWN
NW3 5TG

Your VAT Office telephone number is 01905 855600

Registration Number	Period
454 7108 51	12 XX

You could be liable to a financial penalty if your completed return and all the VAT payable are not received by the due date.

Due date: 31 01 XX

For Official Use

Before you fill in this form please read the notes on the back and the VAT leaflet *"Filling in your VAT return"*. Fill in all boxes in ink, and write 'none' where necessary. Don't put a dash or leave any box blank. If there are no pence write **"00"** in the pence column **Do not** enter more than one amount in any box.

For official use			£	p
	VAT due in this period on **sales** and other outputs	**1**		
	VAT due in this period on **acquisitions** from other **EC Member States**	**2**		
	Total VAT due **(the sum of boxes 1 and 2)**	**3**		
	VAT reclaimed in this period on **purchases** and other inputs (including acquisitions from the EC)	**4**		
	Net VAT to be paid to Customs or reclaimed by you **(Difference between boxes 3 and 4)**	**5**		
	Total value of **sales** and all other outputs excluding any VAT. **Include your box 8 figure**	**6**		00
	Total value of **purchases** and all other inputs excluding any VAT. **Include your box 9 figure**	**7**		00
	Total value of all **supplies** of goods and related services, excluding any VAT, to other **EC Member States**	**8**		00
	Total value of all **acquisitions** of goods and related services, excluding any VAT, from other **EC Member States**	**9**		00

Retail schemes. If you have used any of the schemes in the period covered by this return, enter the relevant letter(s) in this box.

DECLARATION: You, or someone on your behalf, must sign below.

If you are enclosing a payment please tick this box.

I, ...declare that the
(Full name of signatory in BLOCK LETTERS)

information given above is true and complete.

Signature ....Date ....19..............

A false declaration can result in prosecution.

L

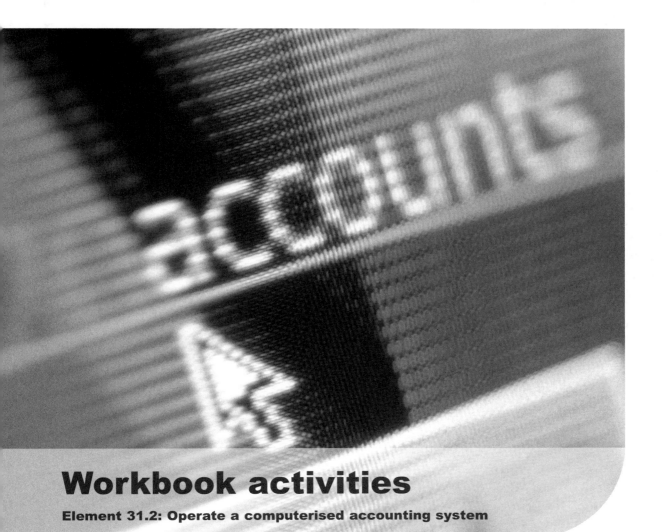

Workbook activities

Element 31.2: Operate a computerised accounting system

This section contains activities which are suitable for use with Chapters 10 to 15 of *Accounting Work Skills Tutorial* from Osborne Books.

The computerised accounting exercises in Chapters 12 to 15 are based on a single business – Fenner Fencing Limited – and are designed to familiarise the student with the second part of the Simulation.

AAT Simulations do not specify any particular accounting program, but the popularity of Sage software makes it an obvious choice, which is why the exercises here are designed to fit well with Sage processes and procedures.

AAT Simulations, at the time of writing, are designed so that students start their input with a completely blank file. This makes for great simplicity, and it also means that there is no longer the need for pre-loaded data, as was the case with previous Osborne Books computer accounting training material.

Further guidance on these exercises is available in the Osborne Books' *Accounting Work Skills Tutor Pack*. Telephone 01905 748071 for further details.

10 COMPUTER SYSTEMS AND ACCOUNTING SOFTWARE

10.1 (a) Describe the 'ledgers' used in a computerised accounting system with which you are familiar, either at work or from your studies.

Do they differ from those used in a manual double entry-system. If so, how do they differ?

(b) State three advantages of a computerised accounting system over a manual double-entry system.

10.2 A new colleague, Julie, starts work with you. You notice at the end of each day that she seems to be spending more time texting her boyfriend than bothering to close down the computer properly or back up her files. On one or two occasions she shuts down her workstation and turns off her printer by flicking the mains switch off at the wall.

'No problem!' she says when she realises that you are watching her 'it's quicker and neater this way!'

What would you say to her?

11 DATA SECURITY

11.1 Your office is shortly to be equipped with a brand-new networked computer system with a central server. It will replace the existing system which comprises five standalone computers. It will mean that each of the new computers will need a unique password of up to eight characters, which can be any combination of numbers and/or letters.

Your manager knows that you are studying computer systems as part of your AAT qualification. She asks you to draw up a list of hints for choosing a password. This list should be designed to contain:

- guidance on good practice – the *do's* of passwords

- things to avoid in choosing passwords – the *don'ts* of passwords

- advice on how to keep passwords secure

11.2 Your office has a networked system of computers, which has been affected badly over the last few weeks by a series of computer viruses. This has resulted in the loss of data and constant disruption to the work flow by computers crashing.

(a) List three simple precautions which could reduce the number of viruses affecting your office computer system.

(b) Describe what action you would take if you realised that your computer had a virus.

12 COMPUTERISED ACCOUNTS – GETTING STARTED

Introduction

The activities in the next four chapters are based on the computerised accounts of a single business – Fenner Fencing Limited.

Fenner Fencing is a company based in Stourcastle, a small country town which serves the rural communities which surround it. Fenner Fencing manufactures and installs fencing, gates and related products to local farms, businesses and households.

The business is run by the Managing Director, Ross Fenner. You work in the Accounts Department and look after the Sage computerised accounting system.

Fenner Fencing offers credit terms of 30 days to all its customers and is VAT registered. All its products are standard-rated for VAT.

The current financial year of the business started on 1 January 2007.

The Tasks

You will be required to:

- set up computerised accounts
- process various transactions involving sales and purchases
- process incoming and outgoing payments
- print out reports at various stages

The activities are very much along the lines of what will be expected in the second part of the Unit 31 Simulation, and will provide useful practice for this assessment.

You may set up the computerised accounting system using any software of your choice. Osborne Books uses Sage Line 50 (Version 11) in its tutorial text and presents the 'answers' to the activities and practice simulations in its Tutor Pack using this software.

12.1 You are to set up the details of Fenner Fencing on the computer. They are:

Financial Year start:	1 January 2007
Company Name	Fenner Fencing Limited
Address	Unit 3, Greenslade Way, Stourcastle ST4 6TG
Telephone	01877 453611
Fax	01877 453286
Email	accounts@fennerfencing.co.uk
Website	www.fennerfencing.co.uk
VAT Reg	GB 0976 2654 34

13 COMPUTERISED ACCOUNTING – CREDIT SALES

13.1   Set out on the next four pages are sales invoices to customers of Fenner Fencing.

The date is 12 January 2007.

You are to:

(a)   open accounts in the Sales Ledger for each customer, using the details and alphanumeric code on each invoice (note also that 30 days terms is standard for Fenner Fencing's customers)

(b)   draw up a batch listing, with totals (net total, VAT and 'total'), for the four invoices

(c)   enter the invoices into the computer, checking your batch totals before saving

(d)   print out a detailed Day Book report for the customer invoices you have input and check the totals with the batch listing

---

INVOICE   FENNER FENCING LIMITED

Unit 3, Greenslade Way,
Stourcastle, ST4 6TG
Tel 01877 453611 Fax 01877 453286
Email accounts@fennerfencing.co.uk
www.fennerfencing.co.uk
VAT Reg GB 0976 2654 34

invoice to		
Oliver Cole & Sons Wood Farm Collingwood ST4 6TF		

invoice no	6275
account	OC001
your reference	675
date/tax point	03 01 07

description	net total
Stock fencing erected	650.00

terms	customer a/c reference	main ledger a/c number
30 days of invoice	OC001	4000
Carriage paid		
E & OE		

net total	650.00
VAT	113.75
TOTAL	763.75

INVOICE

FENNER FENCING LIMITED

Unit 3, Greenslade Way,
Stourcastle, ST4 6TG
Tel 01877 453611 Fax 01877 453286
Email accounts@fennerfencing.co.uk
www.fennerfencing.co.uk
VAT Reg GB 0976 2654 34

invoice to

Wyatt Tool Hire Ltd
7 Newtown Road
Stourcastle
ST1 9CV

invoice no	6276
account	WT001
your reference	10045
date/tax point	04 01 07

description	net total
Repairs to security fencing	270.00

terms
30 days of invoice
Carriage paid
E & OE

customer a/c reference	main ledger a/c number
WT001	4000

net total	270.00
VAT	47.25
TOTAL	317.25

INVOICE

FENNER FENCING LIMITED

Unit 3, Greenslade Way,
Stourcastle, ST4 6TG
Tel 01877 453611 Fax 01877 453286
Email accounts@fennerfencing.co.uk
www.fennerfencing.co.uk
VAT Reg GB 0976 2654 34

invoice to

Victoria Hotel
67 The Parade
Stourcastle
ST2 6HG

invoice no	**6277**
account	**VH001**
your reference	**201206**
date/tax point	**05 01 07**

description	net total
Palisade gate and fencing	800.00

terms
30 days of invoice
Carriage paid
E & OE

customer a/c reference	main ledger a/c number
VH001	4000

net total	800.00
VAT	140.00
TOTAL	940.00

INVOICE

FENNER FENCING LIMITED

Unit 3, Greenslade Way,
Stourcastle, ST4 6TG
Tel 01877 453611 Fax 01877 453286
Email accounts@fennerfencing.co.uk
www.fennerfencing.co.uk
VAT Reg GB 0976 2654 34

invoice to		
Cornwood Stud The Foal Yard Bartisham ST6 4KG		

invoice no	**6278**
account	**CS001**
your reference	**PO1246**
date/tax point	**08 01 07**

description	net total
Rail fencing for new paddocks Delivery charge	1,420.00 80.00

terms
30 days of invoice
Carriage paid
E & OE

customer a/c reference	main ledger a/c number
CS001	4000

net total	1,500.00
VAT	262.50
TOTAL	1,762.50

13.2 Set out on the next two pages are a couple of credit notes issued to customers of Fenner Fencing. The date is 12 January 2007.

You are to:

(a)   draw up a batch listing, with totals (net total, VAT and 'total'), for the two credit notes

(b)   enter the credit notes into the computer, checking your batch totals before saving

(c)   print out a detailed Day Book report for the customer credit notes you have input and check the totals with the batch listing

---

CREDIT NOTE

FENNER FENCING LIMITED

Unit 3, Greenslade Way,
Stourcastle, ST4 6TG
Tel 01877 453611 Fax 01877 453286
Email accounts@fennerfencing.co.uk
www.fennerfencing.co.uk
VAT Reg GB 0976 2654 34

to		
Cornwood Stud	credit note no.	**0072**
The Foal Yard	account	**CS001**
Bartisham	your reference	**PO1246**
ST6 4KG	date/tax point	**10 01 07**

description	net total
Refund of delivery charge on invoice 6278	80.00

reason for credit	customer a/c reference	main ledger a/c number		
refund (telephone call 09/01/07 - terms are carriage paid)	CS001	4000	**net total**	80.00
			VAT	14.00
			TOTAL	94.00

CREDIT NOTE

FENNER FENCING LIMITED

Unit 3, Greenslade Way,
Stourcastle, ST4 6TG
Tel 01877 453611 Fax 01877 453286
Email accounts@fennerfencing.co.uk
www.fennerfencing.co.uk
VAT Reg GB 0976 2654 34

to

Oliver Cole & Sons
Wood Farm
Collingwood
ST4 6TF

credit note number	0073
account	OC001
your reference	675
date/tax point	10 01 07

description	net total
Overcharge on invoice 6275	50.00

reason for credit
refund of overcharge

customer a/c reference	main ledger a/c number
OC001	4000

net total	50.00
VAT	8.75
TOTAL	58.75

13.3 Ross Fenner has asked to see an Aged Debtors Analysis. Print a summary analysis for him as at 12 January 2007.

13.4 Cornwood Stud has asked for an up-to-date statement of account. Print out a statement showing all transactions to date for January 2007.

13.5 Print out a trial balance as at 12 January 2007. Explain what the entries mean.

14 COMPUTERISED ACCOUNTING – CREDIT PURCHASES

In Chapter 13 you have already dealt with the Sales Ledger aspects of computerised accounting. In the activities for this chapter you will deal with Purchase Ledger transactions.

14.1 The date is 12 January 2007. You have received the purchase invoices shown on the next four pages. You are to:

  (a) open accounts in the Purchase Ledger for each supplier, using the details and alphanumeric code on each invoice (note that you receive 30 days terms from these suppliers)

  (b) draw up a batch listing, with totals (net total, VAT and 'total'), for the four invoices

  (c) enter the invoices into the computer, checking your batch totals before saving

  (d) print out a detailed Day Book report for the supplier invoices you have input and check the totals with the batch listing

---

INVOICE

ESTATE TIMBER LIMITED
Woodbury Farm
Martleford, ST6 5FG
Tel 01877 345826 Fax 01877 345887
Email sales@estatetimber.co.uk
www.estatetimber.co.uk
VAT Reg GB 0997 1754 66

invoice to		
Fenner Fencing Limited Unit 3, Greenslade Way, Stourcastle ST4 6TG	invoice no	71833
	account	FF002
	your reference	1762
	date/tax point	02 01 07

description	net total
Assorted posts	750.00

terms	supplier a/c reference	main ledger a/c number		
30 days of invoice			net total	750.00
Carriage paid	ET001	5000	VAT	131.25
E & OE			TOTAL	881.25

INVOICE

Chapman Panels

17 Main Street
Martleford, ST5 2BG
Tel 01877 330472
VAT Reg 0782 1763 99

invoice to

Fenner Fencing Limited
Unit 3, Greenslade Way,
Stourcastle
ST4 6TG

invoice no	**52132**
account	**1873**
your reference	**1765**
date/tax point	**03 01 07**

description	net total
Bow top fence panels	490.00

terms

30 days of invoice

Carriage paid

E & OE

supplier a/c reference	main ledger a/c number
CP001	5000

net total	**490.00**
VAT	**85.75**
TOTAL	**575.75**

Johnson Screws and Fixings

Unit 5, Huckle Estate
Stourcastle, ST2 7SL
Tel 01644 675198 Fax 01644 675166
Email accounts@jscrews.co.uk
www.jscrews.co.uk
VAT Reg GB 0309 1842 11

INVOICE

invoice to

Fenner Fencing Limited
Unit 3, Greenslade Way,
Stourcastle
ST4 6TG

invoice no	4125
account	7232
your reference	1764
date/tax point	02 01 07

description	net total
Assorted fixings	390.00

terms	supplier a/c reference	main ledger a/c number		
30 days of invoice			**net total**	390.00
Carriage paid	JS001	5000	**VAT**	68.25
E & OE			**TOTAL**	458.25

INVOICE

B B Joinery

55 Jubilee Square
Dunsford, DU5 7UC
Tel 01655 330472
VAT Reg GB 1827 2323 22

invoice to		
Fenner Fencing Limited **Unit 3, Greenslade Way,** **Stourcastle** **ST4 6TG**		

invoice no	52132
account	1873
your reference	1766
date/tax point	03 01 07

description	net total
Farm-style gate made to specification	370.00

terms	supplier a/c reference	main ledger a/c number		
30 days of invoice			**net total**	370.00
Carriage paid	BB001	5000	VAT	64.75
E & OE			**TOTAL**	434.75

14.2 Set out below is a credit note received from Chapman Panels in respect of a faulty panel.

The date is 12 January 2007.

You are to enter the credit note into the computer, checking your totals before saving.

Then print out a detailed Day Book report for the supplier credit note you have input and check the accuracy of your input.

Back up your work.

CREDIT NOTE

Chapman Panels

17 Main Street
Martleford, ST5 2BG
Tel 01877 330472
VAT Reg 0782 1763 99

to

Fenner Fencing Limited
Unit 3, Greenslade Way,
Stourcastle
ST4 6TG

credit note no	52132
account	1873
your reference	1765
date/tax point	10 01 07

description	net total
Damaged bow top fence panel	70.00

supplier a/c reference	main ledger a/c number
CP001	5000

net total	70.00
VAT	12.25
TOTAL	82.25

14.3 Print out the following reports for Ross Fenner as at 12 January 2007:

(a) a summary Aged Creditors Analysis

(b) a Nominal Activity Report for account 5000 (Materials Purchased)

(c) a Trial Balance

15 COMPUTERISED ACCOUNTING – PAYMENTS

You have already dealt with the computerised Sales Ledger and Purchases Ledger in Chapters 13 and 14. In the activities for this chapter you will deal with computerised payment transactions carried out by Fenner Fencing Limited.

15.1 The date is 29 January 2007.

You have received two cheques and a BACS remittance advice from three of your customers, settling their accounts. These are shown below, together with notes showing coding details. The cheques will be paid into the bank current account, the BACS payment has been paid into the same account.

Southern Bank PLC
Mereford Branch
16 Broad Street, Mereford MR1 7TR

date *22 January 2007*   97-76-54

Pay *Fenner Fencing Limited* ———————   only

One thousand six hundred and sixty eight pounds 50p ———   **£** *1668.50*

Account payee only

CORNWOOD STUD

S T Allion

123456   97 76 54   68384977

> Account CS001,
> paying invoice 6278
> less credit note 0072

Western Bank PLC
Stourcastle Branch
24 High Street, Stourcastle ST1 7TR

date 23 January 2007   66-10-24

Pay Fenner Fencing Limited ———————   only

Nine hundred and forty pounds only ———————   **£** 940.00

Account payee only

VICTORIA HOTEL

B Fawlty

007289   66 10 24   12546934

> Account VH001,
> paying invoice 6277

BACS REMITTANCE ADVICE

FROM: Wyatt Tool Hire Ltd
7 Newtown Road
Stourcastle ST1 9CV

TO
Fenner Fencing Limited
Unit 3 Greenslade Way, Stourcastle, ST4 6TG

22 01 07

Your ref	Our ref		Amount
6276	10045	BACS TRANSFER	317.25
		TOTAL	317.25

THIS HAS BEEN PAID BY BACS CREDIT TRANSFER DIRECTLY INTO YOUR BANK ACCOUNT AT ALBION
BANK NO 11451778 SORT CODE 90 47 17 FOR VALUE 25 JANUARY 2007

You are to:

(a)   List the cheques and the BACS remittance advice on the form shown below, noting down the customer, account codes needed for input, date of payment, invoice paid and amount received. Then total the amount column.

payments from customers (to bank current account)				
customer	account code	date	invoice reference	amount
			TOTAL (£)	

(b)   Input the payments into the computer (into the bank current account).

(c)   Print out a summary Day Book for Supplier Receipts and agree the Day Book total with the total of the listing form shown above to confirm the accuracy of your input.

15.2 The date is 29 January 2007.

Fenner Fencing is paying two of its suppliers by cheque. You are required to input these payments into the computerised accounting system. The cheques are shown below. The counterfoils have the coding details on them.

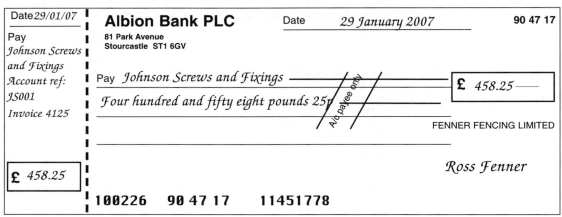

You are to:

(a) Write down the total of the two payments for checking purposes: £...

(b) Input the two payments into the computer (payments to suppliers).

Agree the computer total with the total in (a) above.

(c) Print out a Day Books summary report (Supplier Payments) and, as a final check, agree the total against the total of the two cheques in (a) above to confirm the accuracy of your input.

15.3   The date is 30 January 2007.

You note that on 3 January cheque no 100217 for £165.00 was cashed at the bank to provide funds to restore the petty cash to its imprest level of £200.

Enter a bank transfer (or a journal entry) on the computer from current account to petty cash account to record this transaction.

15.4   The date is 30 January 2007.

The person dealing with the petty cash system hands you three authorised vouchers for input. They have been coded with the necessary account details. They also have notes with them about the VAT on each payment.

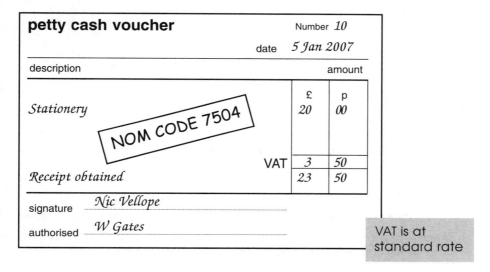

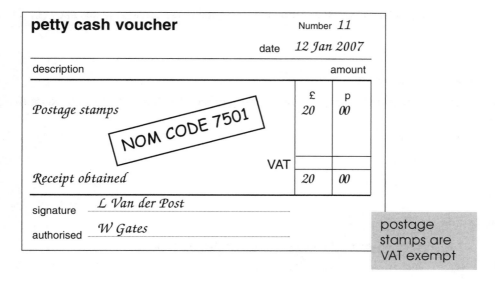

petty cash voucher		Number *12*	
		date *19 Jan 2007*	

description			amount	
			£	p
Floor polish NOM CODE 7801				
		VAT		
Receipt obtained			21	15
signature *Miss Cif*				
authorised *W Gates*				

> VAT is at standard rate, but you will need to work it out - it's not on the receipt!

You are to

(a) Input the three vouchers into the computer system.

Note:

- if you are using Sage this is done through Bank Payments, account 1230

- the account codes on the vouchers are the appropriate expense account codes in Sage

Take care with the VAT element in each case. The notes to the right of the vouchers will tell you what you need to know about the VAT rate.

(b) Print out a detailed Day Book report (Cash Payments) to confirm the accuracy of your input.

15.5 The date is 31 January 2007

As a final check of your accuracy of input of the exercises for Chapters 12 to 15, you are to print out:

(a) a trial balance

(b) an audit trail

15.6 Make sure you

(a) have backed up your data onto a removable storage device

(b) have given the data a unique file name

Workbook activities

Element 31.3: Perform effectively in the workplace

This section contains activities which are suitable for use with Chapters 16 to 22 of *Accounting Work Skills Tutorial* from Osborne Books.

These activities are very practically based in workplace situations and do not always require written answers. In fact a number of the questions could form the basis of group discussion which would widen the perspective of students in preparation for the Simulation.

16 PLANNING AND ORGANISING YOUR WORK

16.1 This activity will give practice in scheduling tasks, an essential part of planning and organising a work schedule.

It is assumed that you are either at work, or know someone at work who could help you, or that you are involved in your own domestic routine. All three scenarios require planning and organising.

You should choose the option which is most appropriate to your circumstances.

You are to:

(a)   Choose a particularly busy day – which in many cases could be a Monday.

(b)   Identify and draw up a rough list of the main tasks that you will have to undertake on that day , either at work or at home.

(c)   Identify the planning aids you could use to help you schedule the tasks and plan out the day (eg diaries, 'to-do' lists, 'sticky' notes on the computer or the fridge).

(d)   Draw up a schedule for that day. A suggested format is shown below.

Name..

Place where the tasks take place ....

Date ....

Time	Task

16.2 Choose a different day from the day chosen in the previous activity.

   (a)   Identify the main tasks (eg six tasks) that you have to carry out.

   (b)   List the tasks in order of priority.

   (c)   Explain why the first two tasks in your list in (b) had the highest priority.

   (d)   Identify a situation from your list where a task with high priority may not be a task which you think is particularly important. Explain why this is the case.

16.3 Think of days which were difficult because things did not go to plan. Give examples of situations during those days where a task had to be done which was:

   (a)   unexpected

   (b)   beyond your capabilities

Explain in each case

   •   what action you took

   •   how the situation was resolved (or was not resolved)

   •   what forms of communication were involved

86

17 WORKING WITH OTHERS

17.1 Imagine that you work in the Accounts Department of a furniture store. Things are not going too well with the staff generally. The management are always promoting the idea of teamwork and the importance of staff members supporting each other, but then they spend long hours isolated in their offices, rarely speaking to the staff.

You find that there are certain types of staff member who really get on your nerves, for example:

(a) Gary in the Accounts Department who often comes in late, badly hung over, and who often makes mistakes with invoices which others have to sort out.

(b) Drew in Sales who is often rude to customers by trying to be funny and cheeky. You have even seen customers walk out of the store as a result of his attitude.

(c) Suzi in the Accounts Department who only has one gear at work, which is very slow indeed. She often fails to meet deadlines.

(d) Terri, who if things get very busy, rings in complaining of a bad cold and 'throws a sicky'.

Explain how these characters affect 'team' performance. If you were in a management role, what action would you take to improve team morale and performance?

17.2 Describe a 'team' situation, eg a work team, a sports team, a family group, in which a major problem has occurred.

Explain how the problem was dealt with, or if it was not satisfactorily resolved, how you think it should have been dealt with.

18 PERFORMANCE, TRAINING AND DEVELOPMENT

18.1   Identify your own training needs. These could relate to in-work training (if you are in work) or to training for a possible career (if you are not currently employed).

State what your goals are (career or otherwise) and work out training targets for achieving those goals.

18.2   Identify the next level of AAT qualification you wish to achieve. Set time and study targets (eg how you are going to study and when) for this next AAT level and explain how you are going to achieve your objectives.

19 & 20   HEALTH & SAFETY ISSUES

Chapters 19 and 20 between them cover the first part of Performance Criterion F of Element 31.3:

Monitor work methods and activities against legislation, regulations and organisational procedures

The single activity here usefully combines the subject matter of the two chapters in one extended task.

Task

Identify a working environment with which you are familiar. It could be your own workplace (if you are in employment), the workplace of a partner or good friend, or it could be your college.

You are to:

(a)   identify some potential Health & Safety hazards

(b)   find out who is responsible for them (it could be the employer/college management/employee)

(c)   identify the legislation which relates to the hazards and explain the precautions that the legislation requires to be taken to avoid harm or injury

21 ACCIDENTS AND EMERGENCIES

Chapter 21 covers the second part of Performance Criterion F of Element 31.3 (the text shown here in bold type):

*Monitor work methods and activities against legislation, regulations and organisational procedures **ensuring that emergency procedures are adequate for potential hazards.***

21.1 Describe an actual (or possible) breach of security in your workplace or college.

Describe what action was (or should be) taken to deal with this hazard.

21.2 Describe an accident which happened at your workplace – or create a fictitious accident – and complete the accident report form shown on the next page.

21.3 You work in a medical research laboratory which has received media coverage for its work on the development of human cloning.

A suspicious package arrives in the post.

What action should be taken to deal with this situation?

Required for activity 21.2 (see previous page)

Accident Report

Full name of injured person _____

Job Title _____ Department _____

Date of accident _____ Time _____

Location _____

Details of accident

Injury sustained

Witnesses
Name   Job title   Department

Action Taken

Further action necessary

Reported by _____ Reported to _____

Signature _____ Date _____

22 MANAGING THE WORK AREA

22.1 Describe your current work area – which may be your workplace or your study area at home.

Draw up a sketch plan to illustrate this work area.

Identify areas which could make this work area

(a) more effective

(b) more efficient

my work area

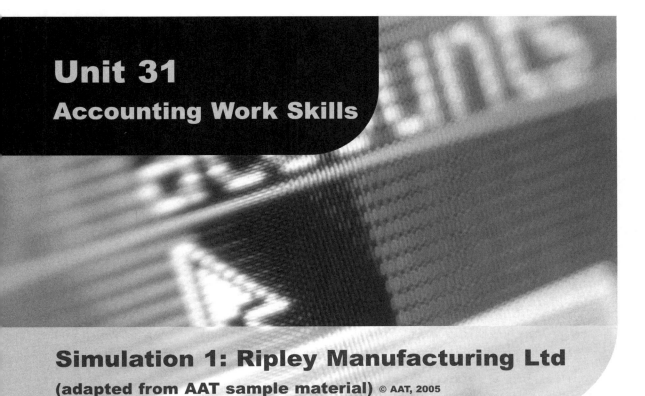

Unit 31
Accounting Work Skills

Simulation 1: Ripley Manufacturing Ltd
(adapted from AAT sample material) © AAT, 2005

Element coverage

31.1 Present financial information for internal and external use.

31.2 Operate a computerised accounting system.

31.3 Perform effectively in the workplace.

Scenario and contents

The Simulation is in three parts, each covering one of the three Unit Elements.

The scenario for the first two parts is based on Ripley Manufacturing, a company which manufactures a product called an 'ampex'.

Part One (pages 94 – 106) involves:

■ preparing a consolidated statement of costs and revenues from accounting data

■ calculating performance indicators relating to this data

■ adjusting the data for the effects of inflation in order to compare two years' data

■ writing a report on the data

■ reporting financial data as part of a grant application process

■ completing a VAT Return (Form 100)

Part Two (pages 107 – 122) involves:

■ processing financial documents using a computerised accounting system

■ printing out reports from a computerised accounting system

Part Three (pages 123 – 128) involves:

■ a one month 'takeaway' project relating to skills required in the work place

SIMULATION 1
RIPLEY MANUFACTURING LIMITED

INTRODUCTION

Your name is Lynsey Jones and you are a trainee Accounting Technician working for Ripley Manufacturing Limited. You report to the company's Accountant, Grace Mbebwe.

Summary of tasks

This section of the assessment is divided into two parts.

■ In Part One, you will be required to perform tasks concerned with the company's accounting year ended 30 June 2005, including preparation of the company's VAT return for the quarter ending on that date. You will be using a spreadsheet package and a word processing package. You will also be completing some of the tasks manually.

Part One should take 90 minutes to complete.

■ In Part Two, you will be required to make entries to a computerised accounting package for transactions occurring in July 2005. You will also be printing out certain reports from the computerised package.

Part Two should take 90 minutes to complete.

The business and structure of Ripley Manufacturing Limited

The company's business is the manufacture and sale of an electronic product called the ampex. The business is organised in three divisions.

1   The Manufacturing Division buys in components and makes sub-assemblies.

2   The Assembly Division receives the sub-assemblies from the Manufacturing Division and also buys in other materials from external suppliers. The division then assembles these components to produce finished ampexes.

3   The Sales and Administration Division receives the finished ampexes from the Assembly Division and sells them to customers. This division is also responsible for all of the administration functions within the company.

Accounts and Reports

All transfers between divisions are accounted for at cost; in other words, there is no inter-divisional profit.

At the end of the accounting year (30 June) the summary cost statements for the Manufacturing and Assembly Divisions, and the summary cost and revenue statement for the Sales and Administration

Division, are consolidated in a standard form to produce a total statement of costs and revenues. In the consolidated statement, the effects of any transfers between divisions must be removed.

Application for grant support

Ripley Manufacturing Limited is located in an area where government incentives are available to manufacturing companies. The management of the company believe they may be able to obtain a grant to help fund the purchase of new manufacturing equipment. Part of your responsibility will be to compile information to support the grant application.

VAT

Ripley Manufacturing Limited is registered as a single entity for VAT. The individual divisions are not registered. Sales of all the company's products are standard-rated to customers within the UK, but the company also makes export sales to other EU countries. These qualify as zero-rated. The company does not import goods or services.

One of your responsibilities is to complete the quarterly VAT return for signature by Grace Mbebwe.

Spreadsheets

Some of the tasks in this assessment require you to access spreadsheet files. These can be downloaded free of charge from the Resources Section of www.osbornebooks.co.uk

Note: if Section 1 of this Simulation is being used for home study practice and a computer is not available, the spreadsheet screens reproduced on pages 98,100 and 101 may be filled in manually, as long as it is realised by the student that this is a temporary measure.

Presenting your work

Unless otherwise stated, all ratios and statistics should be computed and presented to two places of decimals, and all monetary amounts should be stated to the nearest penny.

TASKS: PART ONE

Accounting information

The tasks in Part One relate to the accounts for the year ended 30 June 2005, including the VAT return for the quarter ended on that date.

Task 1

The divisional cost and revenue statements for the year ended 30 June 2005 are shown below, together with additional related information.

Cost statement: Manufacturing Division

Year ended 30 June 2005

		£
	Opening stock of raw materials	61,500
Add:	Purchases of raw materials	457,300
		518,800
Less:	Closing stock of raw materials	77,000
	Total usage of raw materials	441,800
Add:	Factory labour	325,500
Add:	Factory overheads	233,400
	Transfer cost to Assembly Division	1,000,700

Cost statement: Assembly Division

Year ended 30 June 2005

		£
	Opening stock of raw materials	51,300
Add:	Purchases of raw materials from external suppliers	248,700
Add:	Transfer cost from Manufacturing Division	1,000,700
		1,300,700
Less:	Closing stock of raw materials	72,400
	Total usage of raw materials	1,228,300
Add:	Factory labour	313,600
Add:	Factory overheads	332,000
	Total manufacturing cost transferred to Sales and Administration Division*	1,873,900

*Representing the cost of 4,100 completed ampexes transferred

Cost and revenue statement: Sales and Administration Division

Year ended 30 June 2005

		£	£
	Sales		3,771,800
	Cost of goods sold		
	Opening cost of finished goods	139,800	
Add:	Transfer cost from Assembly Division	1,873,900	
		2,013,700	
Less:	Closing stock of finished goods	104,000	
	Total cost of goods sold	1,909,700	
Add:	Sales and administration salaries	539,800	
Add:	Other sales and administration costs	684,400	
	Total costs		3,133,900
	Net profit before taxation		637,900

Additional information

Total capital employed by Ripley Manufacturing Limited:

Year ended 30 June 2005	£11,040,000
Year ended 30 June 2004	£9,412,000

Total staff employed (full time equivalents):

Year ended 30 June 2005	104
Year ended 30 June 2004	95

You are to

Prepare a consolidated statement of costs and revenues for the year.

This is to be done using the spreadsheet file called Ripley Consolidation (available for download from the Resources Section of www.osbornebooks.co.uk (see the next page).

You should print out your completed spreadsheet and hand it in at the end of the assessment along with your other answers.

Remember that you are required to remove from the consolidated totals any transfers made between divisions.

	A	B	C	D	E	F
1	Ripley Manufacturing Limited: Consolidated statement of cost and revenues					
2	Year ended 30 June 2005					
3						
4			Manufacturing	Assembly	Sales & Admin	Consolidated
5			£	£	£	£
6						
7		Sales				
8						
9		Cost of goods sold				
10		Opening stock of finished goods				
11	plus	Total usage of raw materials				
12	plus	Total factory labour				
13	plus	Total factory overheads				
14						
15	less	Closing stock of finished goods				
16		Total cost of goods sold				
17						
18		Gross profit				
19						
20	less	Sales & administration salaries				
21	less	Other sales and administration costs				
22						
23		Net profit before taxation				

Task 2

Using your consolidated figures for the year ended 30 June 2005, and the additional information provided on page 97, calculate the following ratios and statistics, completing the form shown on page 103.

- Gross profit margin for the year

- Net profit margin for the year

- Return on capital employed for the year

- Manufacturing cost per ampex manufactured in the year

- Sales revenue earned per employee in the year

Task 3

Ripley's management have made the following estimates relating to the effects of price inflation on the accounting figures for the year ended 30 June 2005.

- Materials costs have been on average three per cent more expensive than in the previous year.

- Factory labour and overhead costs have been on average four per cent more expensive than in the previous year.

- Sales and administration costs, including sales and administration salaries, have been on average three per cent more expensive than in the previous year.

- Ripley's own selling prices have risen by six per cent on average compared with the previous year.

On the basis of these estimates, re-state in 2005 terms the consolidated figures of costs and revenues for the year ended 30 June 2004, expressing the adjusted 2004 figures to the nearest £.

The unadjusted 2004 figures are contained in the spreadsheet 'Ripley Adjustment' which is shown on the next page. This spreadsheet may be downloaded from the Resources Section of www.osbornebooks.co.uk

You should do your work on the spreadsheet file.

You should print out your solution and hand it in at the end of the assessment along with your other answers.

	A	B	C	D	E	F
1	**Ripley Manufacturing Ltd: Consolidated Statement of Revenues and Costs**					
2	**Year ended 30 June 2004**					
3						
4			**Adjusted**		**Unadjusted**	
5			£	£	£	£
6						
7	Sales					3,388,200
8						
9	Cost of goods sold					
10						
11	Opening stock of finished goods		122,600		122,600	
12	add Total usage of raw materials				644,100	
13	add Total factory labour				624,300	
14	add Total factory overheads				553,500	
15					1,944,500	
16	less Closing stock of finished goods		139,800		139,800	
17	Total cost of goods sold					1,804,700
18						
19	Gross profit					1,583,500
20						
21	less Sales & Administration salaries				517,400	
22						
23	less: Other Sales & Administration costs				592,700	
24						1,110,100
25	Net profit before taxation					473,400

Task 4

Download from the Resources Section of www.osbornebooks.co.uk the spreadsheet Ripley Comparison.

■ Working on the spreadsheet file, enter the actual figures for 2005 (as computed in Task 1) in the column headed Actual 2005.

■ Enter the adjusted figures for 2004 (as computed in Task 3) in the column headed 'Adjusted 2004'.

■ Calculate the variances for each line of the report and enter your results in the column headed 'Variance £'.

■ Each variance should then be expressed as a percentage of the adjusted 2004 figure and entered in the column head 'Variance %'.

Favourable variances should be expressed as positive figures; unfavourable variances should be expressed as negative figures. A variance is favourable if the 2005 figure is an improvement on the adjusted 2004 figure; a variance is unfavourable if the 2005 figure is worse than the adjusted 2004 figure.

You should print out your solution and hand it in at the end of the assessment along with your other answers.

	A	B	C	D	E
1	**Ripley Manufacturing Limited: Comparison of actual 2005 results with adjusted 2004 results**				
2					
3					
4		Actual 2005	Adjusted 2004	Variance	Variance
5		£	£	£	%
6					
7	Sales				
8					
9	Cost of Goods Sold				
10					
11	Sales & Admin Salaries				
12					
13	Other Sales and Admin Costs				
14					
15	Net Profit before Taxation				
16					

Task 5

Using a word processing package, prepare a report (addressed to Grace Mbebwe, and dated 15 July 2005) summarising the variances calculated in Task 4.

Grace prefers a narrative statement of variances, so it is not sufficient simply to submit the tabular report prepared in Task 4.

You should print out your report and hand it in at the end of the assessment along with your other answers. You may wish to use page 104 to draft your report.

Task 6

On page 105 there is an extract from a standard form issued by the grant authority responsible for processing Ripley's grant application.

Complete the form by inserting the accounting figures, ratios and statistics required by the authority. Your answers should be based on the consolidated figures (not divisional figures) for the years ended 30 June 2005 and 30 June 2004 (with no adjustment for changes in prices or costs).

Task 7

The following details have been extracted from the company's day books. All figures are exclusive of VAT.

Sales day book totals: Quarter ended 30 June 2005

	April	May	June	Total
	£	£	£	£
UK sales: standard rated	264,000	298,000	263,000	825,000
EU sales: zero rated	35,900	41,600	52,400	129,900
Total	299,900	339,600	315,400	954,900
VAT on UK sales	46,200	52,150	46,025	144,375

Purchases day book totals: Quarter ended 30 June 2005

	April	May	June	Total
	£	£	£	£
Purchases/expenses	144,000	170,000	163,000	477,000
VAT on purchases/expenses	25,200	29,750	28,525	83,475

A debt of £940, inclusive of VAT, was written off as bad in June 2005.

The related sale was made in August 2004. Bad debt relief is now to be claimed.

You are to

Complete the blank VAT return for that quarter on page 106, ready for signature by Grace Mbebwe. The company pays VAT due by cheque.

ANSWER PAGES: PART ONE

Task 2

Ripley Manufacturing Limited	
Ratios and Statistics for the year ended 30 June 2005	
Gross profit margin for the year	
Net profit margin for the year	
Return on capital employed for the year	
Manufacturing cost per ampex manufactured in the year	
Sales revenue earned per employee in the year	

Task 5

REPORT	
To:	From:
Subject:	
Date:	

Task 6

FINANCIAL INFORMATION IN SUPPORT OF APPLICATION (extracts)

Name of Company _____

Year ended _____

DATA

	Current year		Previous year	
	£	% of sales	£	% of sales
Sales				
Gross profit				
Net profit before taxation				
Total labour and salary costs				
Other costs				
Return on capital employed*				

* Return on capital employed is defined as the ratio of net profit before taxation to total capital employed.

Task 7

<table>
<tr><td colspan="2">

For the period
01 04 05 to 30 06 05
</td><td colspan="2">

SPECIMEN
</td></tr>
</table>

HM Customs
and Excise

RIPLEY MANUFACTURING LIMITED
UNIT 13
LEIGH INDUSTRIAL ESTATE
RIVENDELL
RL5 7ET

Registration Number	Period
578 4060 19	06/05

You could be liable to a financial penalty if your completed return and all the VAT payable are not received by the due date.

Due date: 31 07 05

For Official Use	

If you have a general enquiry or need advice please
call our National Advice Service on 0845 010 9000

Before you fill in this form please read the notes on the back and the VAT leaflet *"Filling in your VAT return"*. Fill in all boxes clearly in ink, and write 'none' where necessary. Don't put a dash or leave any box blank. If there are no pence write "00" in the pence column. **Do not** enter more than one amount in any box.

For official use		£	p
VAT due in this period on **sales** and other outputs	**1**		
VAT due in this period on **acquisitions** from other **EC Member States**	**2**		
Total VAT due **(the sum of boxes 1 and 2)**	**3**		
VAT reclaimed in this period on **purchases** and other inputs (including acquisitions from the EC)	**4**		
Net VAT to be paid to Customs or reclaimed by you **(Difference between boxes 3 and 4)**	**5**		
Total value of **sales** and all other outputs excluding any VAT. **Include your box 8 figure**	**6**		00
Total value of **purchases** and all other inputs excluding any VAT. **Include your box 9 figure**	**7**		00
Total value of all **supplies** of goods and related services, excluding any VAT, to other **EC Member States**	**8**		00
Total value of all **acquisitions** of goods and related services, excluding any VAT, from other **EC Member States**	**9**		00

If you are enclosing a payment please tick this box.

DECLARATION: You, or someone on your behalf, must sign below.

I, ... declare that the
(Full name of signatory in BLOCK LETTERS)

information given above is true and complete.

Signature .... Date ....
A false declaration can result in prosecution.

L

0041633

VAT 100 (half)

TASKS: PART TWO

The tasks in Part Two require you to process accounting transactions occurring in July 2005, using your computerised accounting package.

Task 8

Five sales invoices and a credit note are ready for entry and are shown on pages 109-114.

In the space provided on each document note the customer account code you intend to use and the relevant main ledger code(s).

Task 9

Open accounts for each of the customers. The details needed are on each invoice. Note that the standard terms agreed with credit customers is 30 days net and a credit limit of £20,000. Save your work.

Task 10

Enter each sales invoice and the credit note on to the computer and save your work.

Task 11

Four purchase invoices and a credit note have been received from suppliers and are shown on pages 115 to 119.

In the space provided on each document note the supplier account codes you intend to use and the relevant main ledger code(s).

Task 12

Open accounts for each supplier and save your work.

Task 13

Enter each invoice and the credit note on the computer and save your work.

Task 14

Code and enter on to the computer the journals shown on page 120.

Task 15

Enter the following items on the computer, and then save your work.

Begin by writing the codes you intend to use on each of the documents. Note that money received from customers need not be allocated to specific invoices at this stage.

■ Cheques from customers – see pages 120-121.

■ BACS remittance advice from customer – see page 121.

■ Cheque to supplier – see page 121.

■ Petty cash claim – see page 122.

Task 16

Print out the following items:

■ Statements of account to be sent to customers

■ Sales and sales returns day books

■ Purchases and purchases returns day books

■ Subsidiary sales ledger – aged debtors analysis

■ Subsidiary purchases ledger – aged creditors analysis

■ Trial balance

Task 17

Make a backup of your data onto a removable storage device and label the device appropriately.

Task 18

Close down the computer. Write a note (on page 122) to explain:

■ How you closed down the computer system so as not to cause any damage.

■ How files can be protected using passwords (and why, and how often, passwords should be changed).

■ How files can be protected by appropriate procedures for disk storage.

ANSWER PAGES: PART TWO

Task 8

INVOICE

RIPLEY MANUFACTURING LIMITED

Unit 13, Leigh Industrial Estate
Rivendell RL5 7ET
Tel 01915 765287 Fax 01915 765830
Email accounts@ripley.co.uk
www.ripley.co.uk
VAT Reg GB 578 4060 19

invoice to

Silmar Ltd
35 Rowan Avenue
Bixton
MJ2 5QW

invoice no	21336
date/tax point	04 07 05

description	unit price (£)	quantity	total (£)
Ampexes	920.00	10	9,200.00

customer a/c reference	main ledger a/c number

net total	9,200.00
VAT @ 17.5%	1,610.00
TOTAL	10,810.00

terms
30 days of invoice

Task 8 (continued)

INVOICE

RIPLEY MANUFACTURING LIMITED

Unit 13, Leigh Industrial Estate
Rivendell RL5 7ET
Tel 01915 765287 Fax 01915 765830
Email accounts@ripley.co.uk
www.ripley.co.uk
VAT Reg GB 578 4060 19

invoice to

Bulmers SA	invoice no 21337
2005 Boulevard Raspaille	date/tax point 04 07 05
Chapperville	
Lyons	
France	

description	unit price (£)	quantity	total (£)
Ampexes	920.00	5	4,600.00

customer a/c reference	main ledger a/c number

net total	4,600.00
VAT @ 0%	-
TOTAL	4,600.00

terms
30 days of invoice

Task 8 (continued)

INVOICE

RIPLEY MANUFACTURING LIMITED

Unit 13, Leigh Industrial Estate
Rivendell RL5 7ET
Tel 01915 765287 Fax 01915 765830
Email accounts@ripley.co.uk
www.ripley.co.uk
VAT Reg GB 578 4060 19

invoice to

Parton Plc
22 Lavender Road
Pittsbury
PR7 7FG

invoice no	21338
date/tax point	04 07 05

description	unit price (£)	quantity	total (£)
Ampexes	920.00	6	5,520.00

customer a/c reference	main ledger a/c number

net total	5,520.00
VAT @ 17.5%	966.00
TOTAL	6,486.00

terms
30 days of invoice

Task 8 (continued)

INVOICE

RIPLEY MANUFACTURING LIMITED

Unit 13, Leigh Industrial Estate
Rivendell RL5 7ET
Tel 01915 765287 Fax 01915 765830
Email accounts@ripley.co.uk
www.ripley.co.uk
VAT Reg GB 578 4060 19

invoice to

Bauhaft GmbH
Kaiserallee 215
22516 Hofbach
Germany

invoice no	21339
date/tax point	04 07 05

description	unit price (£)	quantity	total (£)
Ampexes	920.00	10	9,200.00

customer a/c reference	main ledger a/c number

net total	9,200.00
VAT @ 0%	-
TOTAL	9,200.00

terms
30 days of invoice

Task 8 (continued)

INVOICE

RIPLEY MANUFACTURING LIMITED

Unit 13, Leigh Industrial Estate
Rivendell RL5 7ET
Tel 01915 765287 Fax 01915 765830
Email accounts@ripley.co.uk
www.ripley.co.uk
VAT Reg GB 578 4060 19

invoice to

Ruhrheim (UK) Ltd
Ruhrheim House
Lymington Road
Danesbury
SD13 6AR

invoice no	21340
date/tax point	04 07 05

description	unit price (£)	quantity	total (£)
Ampexes	920.00	12	11,040.00

customer a/c reference	main ledger a/c number

net total	11,040.00
VAT @ 17.5%	1,932.00
TOTAL	12,972.00

terms
30 days of invoice

Task 8 (continued)

CREDIT NOTE

RIPLEY MANUFACTURING LIMITED

Unit 13, Leigh Industrial Estate
Rivendell RL5 7ET
Tel 01915 765287 Fax 01915 765830
Email accounts@ripley.co.uk
www.ripley.co.uk
VAT Reg GB 578 4060 19

credit to

Silmar Ltd
35 Rowan Avenue
Bixton
MJ2 5QW

credit note no	215
date/tax point	04 07 05

description	unit price (£)	quantity	total (£)
Return of defective ampex, invoice 21117	920.00	1	920.00

customer a/c reference	main ledger a/c number

net total	920.00
VAT @ 17.5%	161.00
TOTAL	1,081.00

Task 11

invoice EDI LIMITED

Charles House
46 Ryman Road
Jedstown
JW1 1UY
VAT Reg GB 223 7612 49

invoice to

Ripley Manufacturing Limited	invoice no 28761
Unit 13	date/tax point 04 07 05
Leigh Industrial Estate	
Rivendell	
RL5 7ET	

description of goods & services	total (£)
Market research (project ref RM78246)	2,600.00

net total	2,600.00
VAT @ 17.5%	455.00
TOTAL	3,055.00

terms
30 days of invoice

Task 11 (continued)

invoice
Rolled Steel Products Limited

28 Viking Avenue
Studham
CD1 6FG
VAT Reg 553 1213 87

invoice to

Ripley Manufacturing Limited
Unit 13
Leigh Industrial Estate
Rivendell
RL5 7ET

invoice no   1985

date/tax point   04 07 05

description	total (£)
5 Tonnes rolled steel @ £200 per tonne delivered 30 June 2005	1,000.00

supplier a/c reference	main ledger a/c number

net total	1,000.00
VAT @ 17.5%	175.00
TOTAL	1,175.00

terms
30 days of invoice

Task 11 (continued)

invoice	Rolled Steel Products Limited

28 Viking Avenue
Studham
CD1 6FG
VAT Reg 553 1213 87

invoice to

Ripley Manufacturing Limited	invoice no	1999
Unit 13	date/tax point	05 07 05
Leigh Industrial Estate		
Rivendell		
RL5 7ET		

description	total (£)
6 Tonnes rolled steel @ £200 per tonne delivered 1 July 2005	1,200.00

supplier a/c reference	main ledger a/c number

net total	1,200.00
VAT @ 17.5%	210.00
TOTAL	1,410.00

terms
30 days of invoice

Task 11 (continued)

<table>
<tr><td colspan="2">

Invoice

</td><td colspan="2">

Postal Services Limited

</td></tr>
</table>

Invoice	**Postal Services Limited**
	Signia House
	80 Luke Street
	Branduin
	BU8 5TT
	VAT Reg 223 7612 49

invoice to

Ripley Manufacturing Limited	invoice no	412738
Unit 13	date/tax point	04 07 05
Leigh Industrial Estate		
Rivendell		
RL5 7ET		

description	total (£)
Replenishment of postal franking machine	500.00

supplier a/c reference	main ledger a/c number

net total	500.00
VAT @ 17.5%	87.50
TOTAL	587.50

terms
30 days of invoice

Task 11 (continued)

credit note   **Rolled Steel Products Limited**

28 Viking Avenue
Studham
CD1 6FG
VAT Reg 553 1213 87

credit to

| Ripley Manufacturing Limited |
| Unit 13 |
| Leigh Industrial Estate |
| Rivendell |
| RL5 7ET |

credit note no   207

date/tax point   05 07 05

description	total (£)
Overcharge for rolled steel on invoice 1864	120.00

supplier a/c reference	main ledger a/c number

net total	120.00
VAT @ 17.5%	21.00
TOTAL	141.00

Task 14

Journal entries July 2005

	Account code	£	£
Computer equipment at cost		1,125.20	
Computer repairs			1,125.20
To correct error of analysis			
Petty cash		100.00	
Bank			100.00
Withdrawal of cash from bank			

Task 15

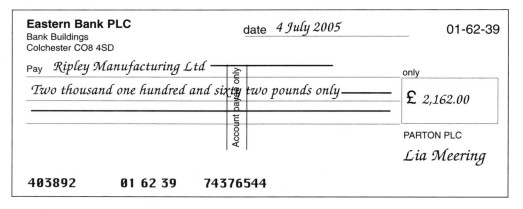

Eastern Bank PLC
Bank Buildings
Colchester CO8 4SD

date *4 July 2005*   01-62-39

Pay *Ripley Manufacturing Ltd* ─────────── only

Two thousand one hundred and sixty two pounds only ─── £ *2,162.00*

PARTON PLC

Lia Meering

403892   01 62 39   74376544

Western Bank PLC
47 High Street, Truro TR1 8NN

date 4 July 2005   25-47-81

Pay Ripley Manufacturing Limited ───── only

One thousand and eighty one pounds only ───── £ 1,081.00

RUHRHEIM PLC

Ben Coates

216645   25 47 81   61145613

Task 15 (continued)

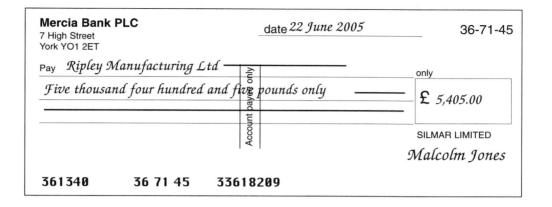

Mercia Bank PLC
7 High Street
York YO1 2ET

date *22 June 2005*   36-71-45

Pay *Ripley Manufacturing Ltd*

Five thousand four hundred and five pounds only   only

£ *5,405.00*

SILMAR LIMITED
Malcolm Jones

361340   36 71 45   33618209

Remitter
Bulmers SA
2005 Boulevard Raspaille
Chapperville
Lyons
France

Beneficiary
Ripley Manufacturing Limited

Date
1 July 2005

REMITTANCE ADVICE

The following sterling amount has been transferred to your bank account in settlement of
invoice 21197 for value 4 July 2005.

£3,680.00

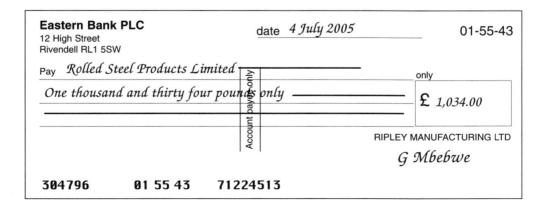

Eastern Bank PLC
12 High Street
Rivendell RL1 5SW

date *4 July 2005*   01-55-43

Pay *Rolled Steel Products Limited*

One thousand and thirty four pounds only   only

£ *1,034.00*

RIPLEY MANUFACTURING LTD
G Mbebwe

304796   01 55 43   71224513

Task 15 (continued)

petty cash voucher			Number 23
		date	4 July 2005
description			amount
		£	p
Train fare (zero rated)		31	00
	VAT		
		31	00
signature	D Jones		
authorised	G Mbebwe		

Task 18

TASKS: PART THREE

Instructions

This assessment is designed to allow you to show your competence in Element 3 of the Accounting Work Skills Unit.

The assessment is to be completed in your own time, using any reference materials you wish.

You must hand in your completed work within one month of the date you begin.

You must complete all the tasks in the assessment.

You should check your work carefully before handing it in.

All of the work must be your own unaided efforts.

Task 3.1

Draw up a to-do list, including the main non-routine tasks that you will have to accomplish in the coming month, including completion of this assessment. As the days go by, prepare a report explaining which of these tasks were accomplished on time, what difficulties arose to cause delays, and how you overcame the difficulties or re-scheduled the tasks. (You will need first to read carefully through the assessment, and then draw up your to-do list incorporating these tasks and others).

Task 3.2

Obtain a copy of the health and safety requirements relating to the organisation you work for, or an organisation you are familiar with (eg the college at which you study). Describe any hazard you have noticed that contravenes the requirements and explain how you would correct the hazard yourself or ensure its correction by others. You must submit a copy of the relevant section of the health and safety requirements and explain clearly why the situation you noticed was in breach of the requirements.

Task 3.3

Obtain a copy of the emergency procedures relating to the organisation you work for, or an organisation you are familiar with. Check whether the procedures cover all of the following situations:

- illness
- accidents
- fires
- other reasons to evacuate the premises, eg bomb threats
- breaches of security

Identify any of the above areas that are not fully covered by the guidance, or confirm that full coverage is given for all areas. You must submit a copy of the emergency procedures, annotated (or with a separate report attached) to show where each of the above areas is covered.

Task 3.4

Imagine that you are in an office when the fire alarm goes off. Looking around, you notice that one of your colleagues is attempting to complete a back-up of her current work before reacting to the alarm. You also notice that a visitor to the office is waiting to be dealt with in reception; he is confined to a wheelchair. Explain what actions you would take to ensure your own safety and that of others.

Task 3.5

Obtain a copy of any accident report forms maintained in the organisation you work for, or an organisation you are familiar with. Complete a report form for any accident you have witnessed, or, if you have not witnessed an accident, complete the form for a fictional accident invented by yourself.

Task 3.6

Draw a plan of your work area on the grid below. (If you are not in employment, draw a diagram of a work area you are familiar with, or invent a fictional work area). Then carry out the tasks that follow the grid.

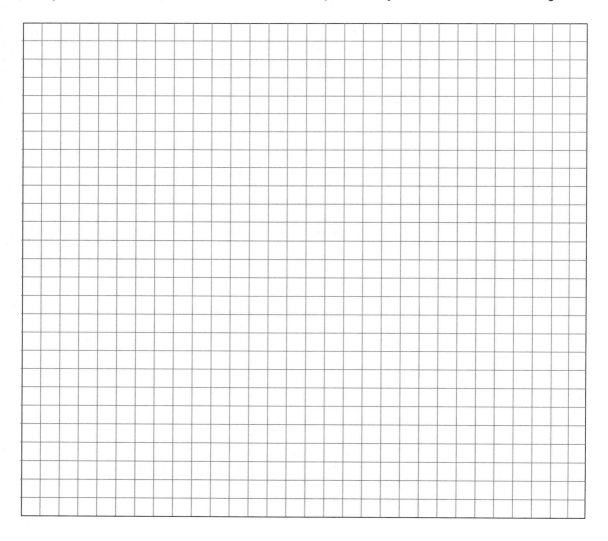

■ Explain how you have organised this area to ensure that you and others can work more efficiently, and to promote a positive image of yourself and your team.

Identify at least one improvement that could be made in this respect.

■ Select any one item of equipment in your work area that is supported by the manufacturer's instructions (eg a computer, or a telephone).

Explain how you use and maintain this equipment in accordance with the manufacturer's instructions.

■ You are provided with a 'Workstation Assessment Form' which is often used in workplaces to assess health and safety conditions relating to work areas. Explore and understand office health and safety regulations relating to workstations by accessing the website www.hse.gov.uk and typing 'workstation' in the search area.

Complete the workstation assessment form supplied on pages 127-128, using the website to help you.

Task 3.7

Choose a day on which you have a heavy workload. (If you are not in employment, choose a day in which you have a heavy study load and a large number of domestic tasks to accomplish).

List the tasks that face you and classify them as urgent or less urgent, with a note explaining why you have classified each task in this way.

Draw up a priority list, showing the order in which you will tackle each task, with an estimate of the time at which you can begin each task. Explain how you would react, and who you would inform, if a very urgent task, requiring about an hour to perform, suddenly arose in the middle of the day.

Task 3.8

Imagine that your boss has repeatedly made last minute demands on your time, causing disruption to your personal schedules. Having decided to discuss the matter with your boss face to face, make notes on:

■ the likely reasons why your boss does this

■ the matters you will want to bring up in the course of the discussion

■ the way you will conduct yourself, taking into account the special nature of face-to-face discussion.

Task 3.9

Make a summarised list of your current job role and career goals.

Identify the gaps between what you currently do, and what you will need to be competent in to achieve your goals.

Explain what training and development you will need to undertake in order to raise your current competence to the required level. (Note that training and development can come in many forms, including self development through reading, observation etc).

SHORT ANSWER QUESTIONS

You may wish to access www.hse.gov.uk for assistance in answering these questions:

1   Identify three health and safety laws that apply in the UK.

2   The employer has a duty under UK law to ensure, so far as is reasonably practicable, the employee's health, safety and welfare at work. What are the employee's duties in return?

3   What do the following abbreviations stand for?

    RIDDOR

    COSHH

4   Give two examples of planning aids that are commonly used in an office environment.

WORKSTATION ASSESSMENT FORM

Workstation location:

Criteria to be assessed	Yes/No
Display screen	
■ Is the display screen positioned in the correct area and the right angle to avoid awkward posture when working at the workstation?	
■ Is it possible to tilt and swivel the screen to position it at the correct height to suit the user?	
■ Is the screen free of reflection and glare?	
■ Is the screen free from flicker?	
■ Is the font size sufficient for the user, and font definition good?	
■ Is there sufficient contrast between the font colour and background to ease readability?	
Notes:	
Keyboard	
■ Is the keyboard separate from the screen?	
■ Can the keyboard be tilted to suit the user?	
■ Is the keyboard design suited to the user needs (eg left-handed etc)?	
■ Is there a wrist rest in front of the keypad?	
■ Is the keyboard clean?	
Notes:	
Work area	
Is there sufficient space around the workstation?	
Is there sufficient work surface to allow for paper and pen work, as well as computer data input?	
Is there sufficient leg room below the work surface?	
Is the leg space free from loose cables and wiring?	
Notes:	

Criteria to be assessed	Yes/No
Chair ■ Is the chair stable? ■ Does it allow the user to sit comfortably in relation to the work desk? ■ Is it possible to adjust the height of the seat, the backrest and angle of the back? *Notes*	
Lighting, reflection and glare ■ Is the lighting adequate for desk work? ■ Can the lighting be adjusted to deal with glare and reflection? ■ Is the workstation fitted with a screen filter to deal with glare? ■ Are there window blinds or other screens to adjust lighting from external sources? *Notes*	
Noise ■ Is the workstation in a noisy environment? ■ Can the noise level be controlled through use of screens etc? *Notes*	
Temperature ■ Can the room temperature be controlled to maintain ambient temperature? *Notes*	

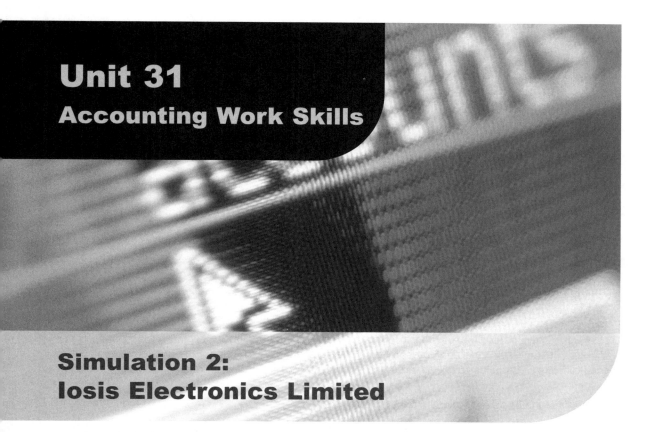

Unit 31
Accounting Work Skills

Simulation 2:
Iosis Electronics Limited

Element coverage

31.1   Present financial information for internal and external use.

31.2   Operate a computerised accounting system.

31.3   Perform effectively in the workplace.

Scenario and contents

The Simulation is in three parts, each covering one of the three Unit Elements.

The scenario for the first two parts is based on Iosis Electronics, a company which manufactures a mobile music player, the 'Electron'.

Part One (Tasks 1.1 - 1.7, pages 130-143) involves:

■   preparing a consolidated statement of costs and revenues from accounting data

■   calculating performance indicators relating to this data

■   adjusting the data for the effects of inflation in order to compare two years' data

■   writing a report on the data

■   reporting financial data as part of an application for bank finance

■   completing a VAT Return

Part Two (Tasks 2.1 - 2.11, pages 144-158) involves:

■   processing financial documents using a computerised accounting system

■   printing out reports from a computerised accounting system

Part Three (Tasks 3.1 - 3.9, pages 159-160) – involves:

■   a one month 'takeaway' project relating to skills required in the work place

SIMULATION 2
IOSIS ELECTRONICS LIMITED

INTRODUCTION

Your name is Jo Wood and you are an accounting technician working for Iosis Electronics Ltd. You report to the company's Accountant, Mike Georgardis. You work in Wokingham, head office of the company.

summary of tasks

This section of the assessment is divided into two parts.

■ In Part One, you will be required to perform tasks concerned with the company's accounting year ended 30 June 2007, including preparation of the company's VAT return for the quarter ending on that date. You will be using a spreadsheet and a word processing program. You will also be completing some of the tasks manually.

Part One should take 90 minutes to complete.

■ In Part Two, you will be required to make entries on a computerised accounting package for transactions occurring in July 2007. You will also be printing out certain reports from the computerised package.

Part Two should take 90 minutes to complete.

the business and structure of Iosis Electronics Limited

The company's business is the manufacture and sale of a mobile music player called the 'electron'. The business is organised into three main geographical divisions:

1   South Division

2   Central Division

3   North Division

Accounts and Reports

All transfers between divisions are accounted for at cost; in other words, there is no inter-divisional profit.

At the end of each month the financial performance statements for the three divisions are consolidated in a standard format head office report to produce a statement of costs and revenues (profit and loss account). When the sales and purchases figures are supplied to head office, any adjustments for stock transfers have already been made.

Application for bank finance

Iosis Electronics Limited is expanding rapidly and the management of the company is in the process of applying for bank finance to help fund the purchase of new manufacturing equipment. Part of your responsibility will be to compile information to support the application for finance.

VAT

Iosis Electronics Limited is registered as a single entity for VAT. Sales of all the company's products are standard-rated to customers within the UK, but the company has not yet started to export to other EU countries, although it has plans to do so. The company does not import goods or services, but sources all its supplies from within the UK.

One of your responsibilities is to complete the quarterly VAT return for signature by Mike Georgardis.

Spreadsheets

Some of the tasks in this assessment require you to access spreadsheet files. These can be downloaded free of charge from the Resources Section of www.osbornebooks.co.uk

Note: if Section 1 of this Simulation is being used for home study practice and a computer is not available, the spreadsheet screens reproduced on pages 133, 136 and 137 may be filled in manually, as long as it is realised by the student that this is a temporary measure.

Presenting your work

Unless otherwise stated, all ratios and statistics should be computed and presented to two places of decimals, and all monetary amounts should be stated to the nearest penny.

TASKS: PART ONE

Accounting information

The tasks in Part One relate to the accounts for the month ended 30 June 2007, including the VAT return for the quarter ending on that date.

Task 1.1

You have just had emailed to you the divisional financial performance figures from the three divisions of Iosis Electronics Limited. They are set out below.

Iosis Electronics Limited
Divisional Financial data for month ended 30 June 2007

	South £	Central £	North £
Sales	90,600	51,500	55,700
Purchases	38,000	13,500	17,500
Opening stock	72,200	42,000	55,000
Closing stock	67,100	39,900	53,500
Wages	12,900	8,700	9,100
Other overheads	25,300	21,200	19,700
Stock Transfers out	10,000		
Stock transfers in		4,000	5,000

You note from the table that £1,000 of stock transferred from South Division to Central Division was in transit at the end of the month and had not been recorded in the books of Central Division. Company policy requires that any stock in transit at the end of the month should be added back to the closing stock of the Division that sent it.

You are to

Prepare a consolidation statement of the financial data of Iosis Electronics Limited for June 2007.

This is to be done using the spreadsheet file 'Iosis Consolidation' (available for download from the Resources Section of www.osbornebooks.co.uk (see opposite page).

Note that no adjustments for <u>recorded</u> stock transfers need to be made to the sales or purchases figures of the three divisions.

You should print out your completed spreadsheet and hand it in at the end of the assessment along with your other answers.

	A	B	C	D	E
1	Iosis Electronics Limited: Consolidation Statement as at 30 June				
2					
3		South	Central	North	Consolidated
4		£	£	£	£
5	Sales				
6	Opening stock				
7	Purchases				
8	Closing stock				
9	Cost of goods sold				
10	Gross profit				
11	Wages				
12	Other overheads				
13	Total overheads				
14	Net profit				
15					

Task 1.2

Using your consolidated figures for the month ended 30 June 2007, and the staffing information shown below, calculate the following ratios and statistics, completing the form shown on page 140.

- Gross profit margin for the month by division and for the group

- Net profit margin for the month by division and for the group

- Sales revenue per employee by division and for the group (to the nearest £)

- Net profit earned per employee by division and for the group (to the nearest £)

Staffing statistics for Iosis Electronics Limited

Staff as at 30 June 2007 (full time equivalent)

South	105
Central	75
North	64
Group	244

Task 1.3

Mike Georgardis is anxious to know how well the company is performing compared with the previous year. He produces figures showing the consolidated Group results for June 2006. They are shown in the table below.

Iosis Electronics Limited
Consolidated Statement for month ended 30 June 2006

	£
Sales	168,000
Opening stock	143,000
Purchases	57,500
Closing stock	137,500
Cost of goods sold	63,000
Gross profit	105,000
Wages	28,500
Other overheads	62,300
Total overheads	90,800
Net profit	14,200

Mike Georgardis asks you to draw up a comparison between the two years. He wants the calculation to be as accurate as possible and asks that you adjust last year's figures for inflation. He tells you that the percentage rises (adjustment factors) for the last twelve months are:

Sales prices	+ 5%
Purchases costs	+ 3%
Wages	+ 4%
Other overheads	+ 5%

Mike provides you with a spreadsheet and asks you to rework the June 2006 figures to allow for the increase in sales prices and purchases and overhead costs.

You are to

Work out the restated figures for June 2006.

This is to be done using the spreadsheet file 'Iosis Adjustment' (available for download from the Resources Section of www.osbornebooks.co.uk) (see the next page).

Print out your solution and hand it in at the end of the assessment along with your other answers.

	A	B	C	D
1	Iosis Electronics Limited: Adjusted Group Statement as at 30 June 2006			
2				
3		June 2006 (actual)	adjustment factor	adjusted figure
4		£		
5	Sales	168,000		
6	Opening stock	143,000		
7	Purchases	57,500		
8	Closing stock	137,500		
9	Cost of goods sold	63000		
10	Gross profit	105000		
11	Wages	28,500		
12	Other overheads	62,300		
13	Total overheads	90800		
14	Net profit	14200		
15				

Task 1.4

Download from the Resources Section of www.osbornebooks.co.uk the spreadsheet 'Iosis Comparison'.

■ Working on the spreadsheet file, enter the actual figures for 2007 (as computed in Task 1.1) in the column headed 'Actual 2007'.

■ Enter the adjusted figures for 2006 (as computed in Task 1.3) in the column headed 'Adjusted 2006'.

■ Calculate the variances for each line of the report and enter your results in the column headed 'Variance £'.

■ Each variance should then be expressed as a percentage of the adjusted 2006 figure and entered in the column head 'Variance %'.

Favourable variances should be expressed as positive figures; unfavourable variances should be expressed as negative figures. A variance is favourable if the 2007 figure is an improvement on the adjusted 2006 figure; a variance is unfavourable if the 2007 figure is worse than the adjusted 2006 figure.

You should print out your solution and hand it in at the end of the assessment along with your other answers.

	A	B	C	D	E
1	Iosis Electronics Limited: Comparison of actual 2007 results with adjusted 2006 results				
2					
3					
4		Actual 2007	Adjusted 2006	Variance	Variance
5		£	£	£	%
6					
7	Sales				
8					
9	Cost of goods sold				
10					
11	Gross profit				
12					
13	Total overheads				
14					
15	Net profit				
16					
17					
18					

Task 1.5

Using a word processing package, prepare a report (addressed to Mike Georgardis, and dated 15 July 2007) summarising the variances calculated in Task 1.4.

The report should include the spreadsheet printout and 'bullet point' comments on the comparative performance of the company over the two years.

You should print out your report and hand it in at the end of the assessment along with your other answers.

You may wish to use the form on page 141 to draft your report.

Task 1.6

On page 142 there is an extract from a standard form issued by the Albion Bank to its customers when they are applying for finance.

Complete the form by inserting the accounting data required by the bank. Your answers should be based on the consolidated figures shown below.

Note that these are the figures for the last quarter (not just for June 2007).

Percentages should be calculated to the nearest percentage.

The form should be prepared for the signature of Mike Georgardis.

Iosis Electronics Limited
Consolidated financial data for quarter ended 30 June 2007

	£
Sales	610,500
Cost of goods sold	230,100
Gross profit	380,400
Total overhead costs	290,500
Net profit	89,900
Capital employed	2,000,000

Task 1.7

The following details have been extracted from the company's day books. All figures are exclusive of VAT.

Sales day book totals: Quarter ended 30 June 2007

	£
UK sales: standard rated	610,500
EU sales: zero rated	nil
VAT on UK sales	106,837

Purchases day book totals: Quarter ended 30 June 2007

	£
Purchases/expenses	410,000
VAT on purchases/expenses	71,750

You are to

Complete the blank VAT return on page 143, ready for signature by Mike Georgardis. The company pays VAT due by cheque.

ANSWER PAGES: PART ONE

Task 1.2

MONTHLY PERFORMANCE INDICATORS FOR IOSIS ELECTRONICS LIMITED				
Date: month ended 30 June 2007				
	South	**Central**	**North**	**Group**
Gross profit margin %				
Net profit margin %				
Sales revenue per employee (£)				
Net profit earned per employee (£)				

Task 1.5

REPORT

To: From:

Subject:

Date:

Task 1.6

Albion Bank Plc

Quarterly Management Accounts

Name of customer:	
Quarter ended:	

Accounting Data Required:

Sales (£)	
Gross profit (£)	
Gross profit %	
Overhead costs (£)	
Net profit (£)	
Net profit %	
Return on capital employed % Note: Formula required $= \dfrac{\text{net profit} \times 100}{\text{capital employed}}$	

Authorised signature of customer

Date

Task 1.7

<table>
<tr><td></td><td colspan="2">For the period
01 04 07 to 30 06 07</td><td colspan="2">SPECIMEN</td></tr>
</table>

HM Customs and Excise

IOSIS ELECTRONICS LIMITED
HERMES HOUSE
AVON INDUSTRIAL ESTATE
WOKINGHAM
WO4 6TF

Registration Number	Period
753 3561 20	06/07

You could be liable to a financial penalty if your completed return and all the VAT payable are not received by the due date.

Due date: 31 07 07

For Official Use

If you have a general enquiry or need advice please call our National Advice Service on 0845 010 9000

Before you fill in this form please read the notes on the back and the VAT leaflet *"Filling in your VAT return"*. Fill in all boxes clearly in ink, and write 'none' where necessary. Don't put a dash or leave any box blank. If there are no pence write **"00"** in the pence column. **Do not** enter more than one amount in any box.

For official use	Description	Box	£	p
	VAT due in this period on **sales** and other outputs	1		
	VAT due in this period on **acquisitions** from other **EC Member States**	2		
	Total VAT due **(the sum of boxes 1 and 2)**	3		
	VAT reclaimed in this period on **purchases** and other inputs (including acquisitions from the EC)	4		
	Net VAT to be paid to Customs or reclaimed by you **(Difference between boxes 3 and 4)**	5		
	Total value of **sales** and all other outputs excluding any VAT. **Include your box 8 figure**	6		00
	Total value of **purchases** and all other inputs excluding any VAT. **Include your box 9 figure**	7		00
	Total value of all **supplies** of goods and related services, excluding any VAT, to other **EC Member States**	8		00
	Total value of all **acquisitions** of goods and related services, excluding any VAT, from other **EC Member States**	9		00

If you are enclosing a payment please tick this box.

DECLARATION: You, or someone on your behalf, must sign below.

I, ... declare that the
(Full name of signatory in BLOCK LETTERS)
information given above is true and complete.

Signature .... Date ....
A false declaration can result in prosecution.

L

0041633

VAT 100 (half)

TASKS: PART TWO

The tasks in Part Two require you to process accounting transactions occurring in July 2007, using your computerised accounting package.

Task 2.1

Four sales invoices and a credit note are ready for entry and are shown on pages 146-150 .

In the space provided on each document, note the customer account code you intend to use and the relevant main ledger code.

Task 2.2

Open accounts for each of the customers. The details needed are on each invoice. Note that the standard terms agreed with credit customers is 30 days net and a credit limit of £10,000. Save your work.

Task 2.3

Enter each sales invoice and the credit note onto the computer and save your work.

Task 2.4

Four purchase invoices and a credit note have been received from suppliers and are shown on pages 151 to 155.

In the space provided on each document note the supplier account codes you intend to use and the relevant main ledger code(s).

Task 2.5

Open accounts for each supplier and save your work.

Task 2.6

Enter each invoice and the credit note on the computer and save your work.

Task 2.7

Code and enter on to the computer the journals shown on page 156.

Task 2.8

Enter the following items on the computer, and then save your work.

Begin by writing the codes you intend to use on each of the documents. Note that money received from customers need not be allocated to specific invoices at this stage.

■ Cheques from customers – see page 156

■ BACS remittance advice from customer – see page 157

■ Cheque to supplier – see page 157

■ Petty cash claim – see page 157

Task 2.9

Print out the following items:

■ Sales and sales returns day books

■ Purchases and purchases returns day books

■ Activity report on customer DFG HiFi

■ Activity report on supplier PPP Components Limited

■ Trial balance

■ Audit Trail

Task 2.10

Make a backup of your data onto a removable storage device, using an appropriate and identifiable file name.

Task 2.11

Close down the computer. Write some notes (on page 158) to explain:

■ the importance of backing up the data you have input

■ the back up policy you use

■ any shortcomings in your back up policy and ways in which the shortcomings could be rectified

ANSWER PAGES: PART TWO

Task 2.1

INVOICE

Iosis Electronics Limited

Hermes House, Avon Industrial Estate
Wokingham WO4 6TF
Tel 01444 856432 Fax 01444 856822
Email accounts@iosis.co.uk
www.iosis.co.uk
VAT Reg GB 753 3561 20

invoice to

Jones Electrical
Unit 5 Deeside Estate
Llangollen
LL2 7FG

invoice no   76521

date/tax point   04 07 07

description	unit price (£)	quantity	total (£)
Electrons	100.00	10	1,000.00

customer a/c reference	main ledger a/c number

net total	1,000.00
VAT @ 17.5%	175.00
TOTAL	1,175.00

terms
30 days of invoice

Task 2.1 (continued)

INVOICE

Iosis Electronics Limited

Hermes House, Avon Industrial Estate
Wokingham RL5 7ET
Tel 01444 856432 Fax 01444 856822
Email accounts@iosis.co.uk
www.iosis.co.uk
VAT Reg GB 753 3561 20

invoice to

DFG HiFI
49 High Road
Stratford
ST4 8BK

invoice no   76522

date/tax point   04 07 07

description	unit price (£)	quantity	total (£)
Electrons	100.00	25	2,500.00

customer a/c reference	main ledger a/c number

net total	2,500.00
VAT @ 17.5%	437.50
TOTAL	2,937.50

terms
30 days of invoice

Task 2.1 (continued)

INVOICE

Iosis Electronics Limited

Hermes House, Avon Industrial Estate
Wokingham WO4 6TF
Tel 01444 856432 Fax 01444 856822
Email accounts@iosis.co.uk
www.iosis.co.uk
VAT Reg GB 753 3561 20

invoice to		
Music Online Ltd Unit 6 Graham Estate Nottingford NG7 7CN	invoice no	76523
	date/tax point	04 07 07

description	unit price (£)	quantity	total (£)
Electrons	100.00	50	5,000.00

customer a/c reference	main ledger a/c number

net total		5,000.00
VAT @ 17.5%		875.00
TOTAL		5,875.00

terms
30 days of invoice

Task 2.1 (continued)

INVOICE

Iosis Electronics Limited

Hermes House, Avon Industrial Estate
Wokingham WO4 6TF
Tel 01444 856432 Fax 01444 856822
Email accounts@iosis.co.uk
www.iosis.co.uk
VAT Reg GB 753 3561 20

invoice to

J H HiFi Supplies
Highbury Court
Bathweston
BA4 8BV

invoice no	76524
date/tax point	04 07 07

description	unit price (£)	quantity	total (£)
Electrons	100.00	15	1,500.00

customer a/c reference | main ledger a/c number

net total	1,500.00
VAT @ 17.5%	262.50
TOTAL	1,762.50

terms
30 days of invoice

Task 2.1 (continued)

CREDIT NOTE

Iosis Electronics Limited

Hermes House, Avon Industrial Estate
Wokingham WO4 6TF
Tel 01444 856432 Fax 01444 856822
Email accounts@iosis.co.uk
www.iosis.co.uk
VAT Reg GB 753 3561 20

credit to

DFG HiFI
49 High Road
Stratford
ST4 8BK

credit note no   834

date/tax point   04 07 07

description	unit price (£)	quantity	total (£)
Return of defective Electron, invoice 76522	100.00	1	100.00

customer a/c reference	main ledger a/c number

net total	100.00
VAT @ 17.5%	17.50
TOTAL	117.50

Task 2.4

invoice AXO advertising

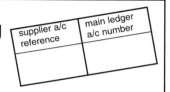

Axo House
56 Georgetown Road
Kingsbury
KI3 7TT
VAT Reg GB 123 7602 46

invoice to

Iosis Electronics Limited
Hermes House
Avon Industrial Estate
Wokingham
WO4 6TF

invoice no   76261

date/tax point   04 07 07

description of goods & services	total (£)
Advertising placements (June 2007)	3,600.00

net total	3,600.00
VAT @ 17.5%	630.00
TOTAL	4,230.00

terms
30 days of invoice

Task 2.4 (continued)

invoice

PPP Components Limited

Unit 6 Felpham Estate
Bilbury
BI6 8GH
VAT Reg 615 1884 26

invoice to

Iosis Electronics Limited
Hermes House
Avon Industrial Estate
Wokingham
WO4 6TF

invoice no   9844

date/tax point   04 07 07

description	total (£)
F665D cards as per contract 310507	2,750.00

supplier a/c reference	main ledger a/c number

net total	2,750.00
VAT @ 17.5%	481.25
TOTAL	3,231.25

terms
30 days of invoice

Task 2.4 (continued)

invoice

PPP Components Limited

Unit 6 Felpham Estate
Bilbury
BI6 8GH
VAT Reg 615 1884 26

invoice to

Iosis Electronics Limited	
Hermes House	
Avon Industrial Estate	
Wokingham	
WO4 6TF	

invoice no   9851

date/tax point   05 07 07

description	total (£)
H7655 cards as per contract 310507	750.00

supplier a/c reference	main ledger a/c number

net total	750.00
VAT @ 17.5%	131.25
TOTAL	881.25

terms
30 days of invoice

Task 2.4 (continued)

Invoice	RR Telecom
	Communication House
	Heasington Road
	Woodstock
	WO2 7CF
	VAT Reg 119 4344 91

invoice to

Iosis Electronics Limited	
Hermes House	
Avon Industrial Estate	
Wokingham	
WO4 6TF	

invoice no	82727
date/tax point	04 07 07

description	total (£)
Telephone contract 98393 (June 2007)	874.00

supplier a/c reference	main ledger a/c number

net total	874.00
VAT @ 17.5%	152.95
TOTAL	1,026.95

terms
30 days of invoice

Task 2.4 (continued)

credit note

PPP Components Limited

Unit 6 Felpham Estate
Bilbury
B16 8GH
VAT Reg 615 1884 26

credit to

Iosis Electronics Limited
Hermes House
Avon Industrial Estate
Wokingham
WO4 6TF

credit note no   442

date/tax point   05 07 07

description	total (£)
Defective cards G7632 on invoice 9826	240.00

supplier a/c reference	main ledger a/c number

net total	240.00
VAT @ 17.5%	42.00
TOTAL	282.00

Task 2.7

Journal entries June 2007

	Account code	£	£
Electricity		453.88	
Gas			453.88
To correct error of analysis			
Petty cash		250.00	
Bank			250.00
Withdrawal of cash from bank			

Task 2.8

Mercia Bank PLC
12 High Street
Stratford CO8 4SD

date *30 June 2007*   36-77-06

Pay   *Iosis Electronics Ltd* ——————————————

One thousand two hundred and fifty five pounds only ——— only

£ *1,255.00*

DFG HIFI

J I Sparks

Account payee only

045631   36 77 06   12876451

Western Bank PLC
12 The Parade, Nottingford NO1 2CD

date 28 June 2007   25-46-22

Pay   Iosis Electronics Limited

Two thousand and ninety five pounds only ——————— only

£ 2,095.00

MUSIC ONLINE LIMITED

R Patel

Account payee only

855406   25 46 22   20986734

Task 2.8 (continued)

BACS REMITTANCE ADVICE

FROM: J H HiFi Supplies
Highbury Court
Bathweston BA4 8BV

TO
Iosis Electronics Limited
Hermes House, Avon Industrial Estate, Wokingham, WO4 6TF

01 01 07

Your ref	Our ref		Amount
76503	4563	BACS TRANSFER	250.25

TOTAL   250.25

THIS HAS BEEN PAID BY BACS CREDIT TRANSFER DIRECTLY INTO YOUR BANK ACCOUNT AT
SOUTHERN BANK NO 11451778 SORT CODE 09 22 07 FOR VALUE 4 JULY 2007

Southern Bank PLC
12 High Street
Wokingham RL1 5SW

date *12 July 2007*

09-22-07

Pay *RR Telecom* — only

One thousand and twenty six pounds 95p —

Account payee only

£ *1,026.95*

Iosis Electronics Limited

M Georgardis

145398   09 22 07   11451778

---

petty cash voucher

Number *75*

date *4 July 2007*

description		£	p
Stationery: envelopes		16	00
	VAT	2	80
		18	80

signature   *J Wood*

authorised   *J Carragher*

Task 2.11

TASKS: PART THREE

This part of the assessment is designed to allow you to show your competence in Element 3 of the Accounting Work Skills Unit. It is to be completed in your own time and must be handed in within one month of the date you begin. You must complete all the tasks in the assessment, and all the work must be your own.

Task 3.1

Draw up a plan for the completion of this 'Part Three' project. Your time scale is one month. The plan should include:

- a list of the tasks involved

- a draft timetable for the completion of the work

- a summary of the resources you will need (eg materials and people to contact)

Identify any areas which you think will prove difficult and make a note of the ways in which you will deal with them.

Task 3.2

Identify the Health & Safety legislation that applies to your workplace or college, or the workplace of a friend. Explain what you would do if you discovered a breach of Health & Safety regulations (the breach could be a real event you have experienced or a fictional one). Describe the breach and the ways in which it contravenes the regulations.

Task 3.3

Obtain a copy of the procedures relating to a fire at your workplace (or place of study) and describe in your own words what action should be taken in the event of a fire.

Task 3.4

Imagine that you are walking down a corridor with a colleague who slips on a wet floor that has just been cleaned. Your colleague badly twists his/her ankle so that he/she is unable to walk on it. What action would you take? (see also Task 3.5).

Task 3.5

Complete an accident report (see page 90 for a sample format) for the accident in Task 3.4. Make up details such as names and dates as appropriate.

Task 3.6

Draw a plan of your work area. If you are not in employment, draw a diagram of a work area you are familiar with, or invent a fictional work area. This work area should include a computer workstation (add one if your work area does not include one).

Describe improvements you could make to the way the area is laid out to ensure that you and others can work efficiently.

Assess how well the computer workstation fulfils Health & Safety regulations and make suggestions for improving the way in which the workstation is set up.

Task 3.7

Imagine you work as an assistant in the accounts department of a chain of shops. One of your weekly tasks is to compile a consolidated sales and stock report covering all the shops in the group.

You are having a problem in completing the report because one of the shop managers is always late in emailing you the figures for his shop.

What action could you take to resolve this problem?

Identify the various stages this process could take.

Task 3.8

Find a job advert for an accounting position you would like to apply for as a next step in your career. This applies whether or not you are currently in employment.

Request an application form and a job description.

Assess your current abilities (ie what you can do) and identify the training and development you need for you to be competent to do this job. State how you will develop the new skills required.

Task 3.9

Refer to Task 3.1 and your plan for completion of this project.

Assess your success in keeping to this plan and describe how you monitored the plan and how often.

Describe situations where:

■ you had to amend the plan

■ you had to change your priorities because of unexpected events or changes in workload

SHORT ANSWER QUESTIONS

1   Identify three laws that relate to discrimination in the workplace.

2   Identify three different ways in which you could communicate with a colleague about a supplier invoice query.

3   Identify three duties of employees under the Health & Safety at Work Act.

4   Identify three forms of harassment that could occur in the workplace.